H/93

Chronicles of Courage

CHRONICLES OF COURAGE

Very Special Artists

■

JEAN KENNEDY SMITH
AND
GEORGE PLIMPTON

RANDOM HOUSE NEW YORK

Library of Congress Card Catalogue Number: 89-43549
ISBN 0-394-57003-0

Manufactured in the United States of America
24689753
First Edition

For Steve,
Stephen, William, Amanda, and Kym

I am most grateful to Lindsey Sheehy for her tireless work and research for this book. My thanks to Edie Ferrante for her transcriptions of the taped interviews and to Amy Gurin, who assisted with administrative support throughout.

I would also like to make a special dedication to the many Very Special Arts participants around the world who have shared in our programs and who have given the world so much wonder and delight.

—JEAN KENNEDY SMITH

We never know how high we are
Till we are called to rise;
And then, if we are true to plan,
Our statures touch the skies.

The heroism we recite
Would be a daily thing
Did not ourselves the cubits warp
For fear to be a king.

—EMILY DICKINSON

Foreword

■

ROBERT COLES

In the mid-1950s, after I finished medical school and began my training in pediatrics, polio was a much-feared disease that suddenly, out of nowhere, would strike particular communities. And that was what happened in Boston during the summer of 1956. I was working at Massachusetts General Hospital, and would soon be at Children's Hospital. Dozens of children came to both hospitals, and by no means all of them left alive or in relatively normal condition—that is, able to use their arms and legs, or to breathe without the assistance of iron lungs. I can still remember some of the conversations I had with those children and their parents, conversations that were in fact efforts on the part of young people and their elders to come to terms with tragedy, to understand, insofar as it was possible to do so, the purpose and meaning of life. Most of all I remember the words of one ten-year-old girl, whose legs were paralyzed: "I just hope I can do the best job when I leave the hospital." I asked her what she meant. She had no trouble offering me an immediate explanation: "My granny said we have our time here to make God smile; I hope I can even get Him to laugh and laugh sometimes! I'll try my best."

She seemed all too hopeful about the time ahead of her, and I was doubtful, not only about her medical prospects but also, in view of some of her remarks, like those I've just quoted, about her psychological future. When would the denial she had mobilized begin to wane? When would she stop being so tenaciously upbeat and hopeful and come to acknowledge how gloomy, sad—and, yes, angry—she must surely feel as a consequence of the singularly bad luck fate had visited upon her? When would she become more realistic, more inclined to face the exact dimensions of her now crippled and vulnerable existence? Such questions might prompt the reader to wonder not only about that child but also about the doctor attending her, whose troubled mind seemed so willing, anxious even, to emphasize the melancholy aspect of things, so eager to call upon psychology and psychiatry to aid him in his darkly skeptical diagnosis. But doctors hold the upper hand in such matters: We are the ones who, in fact, own those psychological and psychiatric terms, and all too often we find ourselves using them as we please, unfortunately not stopping often enough to bow our heads in grateful acknowledgment of life's mysteries, not the least of which is the astonishing capacity many people have to make the best of their troubles, even to find a redemptive outcome in the suffering and pain that has befallen them.

The stories this book offers us keep reminding me of that ten-year-old girl, who grew up to become an exceptionally talented cellist and schoolteacher. Again and again in the pages that follow we find men and women with plenty of reason to feel downcast, to wonder moodily and cynically about the purported significance of life, showing themselves able to muster strength in the face of adversity, willful energy in the face of any number of obstacles. Moreover, each of these individuals has found that a particular talent, exercised with determination and persistence, can be the pathway to a life of accomplishment. As we read about them, we feel respect, even awe—and, what is more, find ourselves hoping to learn from them, because they have learned important lessons about this existence to which we are all called at birth—lessons some of us, healthy as we are, have trouble mastering. As the girl I mentioned earlier said to me, "Maybe my legs were told to stop running me all over the place so that I could stop and find out who 'me' is." By this time she was almost thirteen, naturally introspective in the way adolescents can so often be, yet I recognized that her so-called impairment was working to broaden her sense of reality, to awaken moral reflection, to grant her a breadth and depth of vision with respect to the one and only life she would have. So it has been, too, for many of the men and women we meet here, with Jean Smith's inspired, thoughtful, and sensitive help. She has known to seek for wisdom among people some of us either overlook or, through our own pitiable—if not downright tragic—denial resolutely fail to acknowledge as worthy of the admiring attention and respectful gratitude this book offers. One by one, these brave and resourceful people tell us of their self-discovery and self-affirmation through their work and their actions rather than dwelling on their inner turmoil.

"Polio for me means centuries of time I'd otherwise never have had with Brahms and Prokofiev," the young woman quoted earlier told me in 1968, when I returned to Boston after spending almost a decade in the South. I marveled and admired her wide-ranging achievements, both musical and personal, but most of all I noticed the extraordinary radiance in her face—a wide-eyed openness to others, to human experience as she took part in it, observed it, contemplated it. Nor is she alone. She has many colleagues—those hardworking, gifted people whose appearance in this book will become for us an enduring and collective presence: They will be admitted to our minds as advisers and exemplars who have lived remarkable lives against no small odds.

This is a book that shows us what the human spirit can do, no matter the difficulties placed in our path. As I encountered these extraordinary people, learned their stories, tried to absorb the impact of their testimonies, I kept remembering a phrase of Tolstoy's, one my mother used when she met someone whose character and personal attributes were strikingly worthwhile. "That is a person with 'a large soul,' " she would say. And they await the reader, in this book: a number of large souls, ones encountered by an interviewer wise enough and patient enough to wish to make their acquaintance and, in turn, enable us to do likewise.

■

CONTENTS

Appendices

■

INTRODUCTION

In 1974, when I was a member of the board of the Kennedy Center Education Committee, we discussed at length the importance of arts programs in the schools and how an awareness of the arts can help children express themselves, develop their confidence, use their imagination, and inspire their creativity—in short, give their life meaning in ways that would nurture and challenge their spirit long after they had left school and other lessons in class had been forgotten. How could we do that? We also wanted to reach out through the arts to children and adults with disabilities, who need these programs even more desperately.

Out of these discussions came Very Special Arts. It is a program of great importance to our family, because Rosemary, my oldest sister, was born with mental retardation. We were always encouraged by our parents to bring her everywhere with us—sailing and swimming, to dances and movies. We loved her very much, and we knew that life was especially difficult for her because opportunities for creativity and expression were rare.

Very Special Arts began modestly, with three arts festivals. At these events, people with disabilities met to display and share their art with others. Today, Very Special Arts is present in all fifty states and has affiliates in fifty-five other nations. We have now held over eight hundred festivals, involving two million people in our programs throughout the world.

We sponsor projects in theater, dance, music, painting, sculpture, and many other forms of artistic expression. Our programs are mainstream, involving extensive interaction between disabled artists and other artists. Our goal is not to create one-time experiences, but to foster the lasting values of community and sharing in ways that the arts can uniquely provide. We want to demonstrate that "disabled" does not mean "unable," and that all of us can express ourselves beautifully through the arts, if only we are given the chance.

The artists in this book had that chance. As I visit our arts festivals, I am constantly impressed by the remarkable people whose talents shine through, despite their great disabilities. Tony Melendez plays his guitar with his feet; Chuck Close paints with a brush strapped to his hand; Alison Sheen lost her sight at the age of thirty, yet still participates in dance programs.

When I set out to discover the stories of these artists, I expected to find some who complained or expressed rage and bitterness about their fate. But I was wrong. Their lives are marked by dignity, hope, enormous courage, and laughter. They are artists experiencing the joy of creativity, enriching their own lives, and inspiring us all with a new sense of pride in our common humanity. Hear them in their own words.

—Jean Kennedy Smith

INTERVIEWS

■

■

PAMELA SPURLOCK BOGGESS

A talented artist and art teacher from West Virginia, Pamela Boggess's work was selected for the Call to Rise exhibition sponsored by Very Special Arts. In 1987, she received the Very Special Arts Outstanding Educator Award, which recognized her innovative teaching program for children. The year before, she had served as Miss Wheelchair America. Beautiful, dynamic, she was extraordinarily forthcoming in our conversation about her life, her work, and her disability—it was truly an inspiration to have had the chance to meet her.

Pamela Spurlock Boggess:

I have my own van, and a lift. I drive everywhere and anywhere. I've driven to Florida. I have plans to go to Albuquerque this summer with a friend and my two children. It's all in how you look at it.

I'm raising two children as a single parent. My ex-husband was in a train accident just before our divorce was final and he broke his neck. He came within a gnat's whisker of being a quadriplegic himself.

When I got sick we had been married eight years. He hung around for a while, but he just couldn't make it. He is not an emotionally strong person. That's where I compensated in our relationship. I was very strong emotionally. I handled all the financial parts of our relationship. I kept us together. He went out and worked and did the manly thing.

In a way, it's a lot easier on me that he is gone. I don't have his emotional needs to take care of. I have a lot more to do for myself, and to take care of the children—my baby was a year old when I became paralyzed. My son was four. He thinks he remembers me walking. My daughter sees pictures of me standing and thinks it's my twin sister. She doesn't remember—there's no way she could remember. At the mall, she just holds on to my chair—never wanders off, never even begins to get crazy like some kids do. She just sticks right by my side. It's as though she knows Mom can't go chasing her down, and she'd better stick close to home.

My son's very proud of me. He can't wait for me to show up at school so he can show off. I mean the little things—"She's got a great horn on this chair; watch what she can do with it."

I did a lot of reading during those first four or five months after I got sick. That helped me realize that these things happen regardless of whether you're a good or a bad person. You don't have things to blame. I wasn't in an accident. I didn't do something stupid, unless it was breathe the air. I had cancer. There was nothing anyone could do about those genes deciding to do their thing and become active—nothing! Even if they had diagnosed me ten years earlier, there was still nothing anyone could have done.

I had a couple of choices, and because I had small children, I decided to go with the surgery rather than chemotherapy. The children gave me a reason to be here. I didn't pray to God that I would walk. I forgot about that part. Had I prayed to God that I could walk, maybe I would be walking now. I don't know. But I prayed that I would be there to raise them. I just wanted to have an influence on them. Knowing their father's emotional state, living with him for the years that I did, I knew someone would replace me very quickly. That didn't bother me. I wanted another woman to be on hand to have an influence on the children if I couldn't be there. But, of course, I preferred my own influence. I have a lot of confidence in myself, my views, and my ways of doing things—I thought I'd have an important impact on their lives. And, perhaps, on other people's lives.

I had eight days to decide. I was paralyzed, technically, anyway. I could not move out of my bed. The cancer was killing me. They told me there was a 20 percent chance the operation might work, advanced as my cancer was. The steroids had me bloated. I couldn't eat, I couldn't sleep . . . I was just physically miserable. I had lost function, technically, from the waist down. I could not walk. I had no bladder or bowel control. I couldn't get out of my bed. I could still sit up better than I can now, because I had muscle control from about the waist up. But I was paralyzed, and becoming more paralyzed every day. And the thoughts of the cancer being in my body and climbing up the spinal cord to my brain, where it would manifest itself in a brain tumor and I would die—either suffocate from paralysis of the nerves that take care of breathing and the chest muscles, or a brain tumor, whichever got me first—made up my mind for me: "Let's take it out, and see what happens."

My fifth anniversary of the operation is either March 29 or 31—I can't remember. I've done all these things in between. I think I made the right choice. My kids are going to remember me now. If I had gone ahead and checked out at that time, my baby wouldn't have known me from Adam . . . he'd have just had my picture, and that would've been it.

After the operation, the babies got to visit, and sit on the floor, and come to physical therapy. I took them around in a wheelchair, let them ride and sit on my lap. I acquainted them with the wheelchair and the fact that I would no longer be standing up, that things would be a little bit different, but that I was going to be able to take care of them eventually. I was going to have to learn different ways of doing things to be able to accommodate them.

There are stages you go through. I went through every one of them. Depression. What good am I, what can I do? But, thank goodness, I had the foresight to say to Dr. Allen, "Do not interfere with my hands. If you can do the operation and leave me the use of my hands so I can sit up and do my artwork and further that, I'll be okay. I know I'll be okay. I don't have to play tennis anymore. I don't have to play softball. I don't have to run. I can handle it."

There are times when my right hand does not function correctly. I have some nerve damage in my shoulder and down my arm, so my hand'll just kind of curl up, and I have to drink and eat with my other hand for a while. Fatigue brings that on. Extreme fatigue. When I'm getting a kidney infection, which I'm prone to, that's one of the signs. So I go to bed for a while—and I just stop. I rest. I start taking my antibiotics, and I drink an awful lot. I really like beer now! I never drank beer before in my life, and now I drink beer!

The children are very adjusted to the disability. At the time of the operation, my daughter—it just broke my heart at the time—was learning to walk, and was tickled to death with herself. The kid was verbal at ten months. So once she got the motor control and started walking, she decided she was going to teach *me* how to walk. She said, "Mommy, it's real easy. You just pick your leg up and go like this." And she would do it. She said, "When you get little like me, you'll be able to walk. . . ." That's how she saw it.

Now, they help me in more practical ways. First thing, when we're going to a new place, my son asks, "Mom, can you get in? Is there a ramp here? Are we going to have any problem? You want me to go in and get someone to carry your chair?" This is a nine-year-old. When we stop at the store, I'll give him a list— just out of convenience to keep from transferring into my wheelchair and getting out of the van and going in the store. He can take twenty or thirty dollars and run into the IGA store in our area, and pick up anything I need. He's very good at it. He and Jenny—nine and six years old—go in there with the money in their pockets and their list, and they push the cart around, and they look like little miniatures of big shoppers, you know? "Well, let me see—she said Folger's coffee. Okay." And they pick it out and put it in the cart.

The boy gets a little frustrated that I can't play basketball, and that I can only throw and catch baseballs. We do play Wiffleball, and I can hit the Wiffleball—but then someone else runs for me.

I have someone come in every two weeks to clean. Hit the high spots, and the real low spots. I have a friend who's around a lot. He loves to cook. So that's a real treat for us. But I'm doing it on my own. My mom comes over once or twice a week and visits, and maybe she'll catch the laundry up if I'm behind. Or help change the sheets—that's a little bit of a hassle for me. But other than that, we get the ironing board out and iron our clothes, and we do our laundry, and we take care of the cats. We've made adjustments . . . I have a dishwasher, because your armpits get real wet when you sit below the sink. And I hate doing dishes anyway. I can use my disability as an excuse at times, not to do those things that are unpleasant—like washing dishes. So when we have our family gatherings now, I don't do dishes. My sisters take care of that. But I do help to set the table, and I prepare food. I'm expected to do my share. When we get together, there's between sixteen and twenty people, with all the kids and grand-kids and sons-in-law and so on and so forth. Once it gets *too* crowded in the kitchen, I'm more than happy to get out of there. I'm just not a kitchen person.

Immediately after the operation I went back to my artwork and teaching. Always, always, since I was very small, I wanted to be an artist. This is what I feel comfortable doing, and I do it well. Lord knows, after fifteen years of study, maybe I can really be a professional artist. Since the onset of my disability, I actually do better work. It is more from the soul.

I got involved immediately with community work. I participated in the Miss Wheelchair West Virginia pageant and won Miss Wheelchair West Virginia within eighteen months of becoming paralyzed. You're judged on your ability to speak publicly, how you present yourself and can represent the disabled community—not just mobility-impaired people, but all people with disabilities. I can talk! I definitely can talk! I did! It was a wonderful experience. Becoming involved publicly gave me the boost that I needed at the time—to be able to look at myself in the wheelchair and not get upset. Physically, I'm very different now from what I was when I was standing up. It bothers me at times, but actually a lot of people would like to look as good as I do in a wheelchair, only they're *not* in a wheelchair. So I take some consolation in that. I was able to go to the Miss Wheelchair America pageant, and the people whom you meet, the inspiration you receive from other people in your situation—it helps. Perhaps I can help someone who's been in their home for the last twenty years, unable to get out, afraid to face the public.

It is not easy. The stares that I get, just rolling down the mall taking my kids trick-or-treating. People in wheelchairs don't have kids. "What do you mean, those are *your* kids?" The things they can say are amazing. They look you in the face and say, "You have kids? What are you doing with kids?" I say, "Well, I'm doing very well with kids, thank you. Look at them—they look pretty good! I love my kids, like anyone else."

A lot of these people are scared. The elevator door will open, and they'll wait for a different elevator if I'm in there in my wheelchair—they won't get on the elevator with me.

But kids are the greatest. Kids are wonderful, they walk right up to you. They'll run up and say, "Did you break your legs? Are you hurt? Why can't you walk?" Different questions. From the heart, and they're sincere. I don't mind answering them. My simplistic answer is: "My legs don't work, so I'm in the wheel-chair." No problem. No big deal. They can accept that answer. It makes sense. *Her legs don't work.* But their moms, most of the time, grab their arms—"Billy, no! Leave her alone! Don't stare!" They make a big deal of it. If they would let the children satisfy their curiosity, they would grow up with less fear, fewer questions about people who are different. Because, really, that's all I am: a little bit different. I function on most levels like anyone else. Mobility-wise, I don't. That's the only level. So I am different in that respect only. I'm a contributing human being to our society. For the most part, I contribute more than an awful lot of people out there who don't bother with community service, who don't bother with interaction with the education of our children, and all those things. I really feel that if we educate our children in the primary schools, on the kindergarten level, get them used to seeing people like me, there'll be less animosity—fewer questions when they get older. The architects will automatically include mobile accessibility in their drawings for buildings. Structural barriers will be gone. It's like a filtering system.

The children at my elementary school look at me and accept me for what I am. I am their teacher. I am in authority when they're in my classroom. It doesn't bother them that I can't lean over and pick up papers when I drop them. They know that. *They* pick them up. "Here, Ms. Boggess." No problem. It's automatic. They realize, I think, that I'm creative, that I provide them a service they love. And they really appreciate it. But I don't walk. No big deal. That's it.

I've been semiambidextrous all my life. I sit and talk to my students and write with either hand on the board. Blows their minds. Anyone can do it—you just have to practice. You know, left brain–right brain, and all that good stuff.

At school we're making handmade papers at the elementary level. We're doing silkscreens and linoleum block prints. All of the different media are covered. On TV this little boy—the cutest little boy you ever saw, no teeth in the front, first grader—when they asked him, "What is it you like about Mrs. Boggess being your teacher?"—he looked at me and just grinned. He said, "I just love her because she lets us do all these neat projects and stuff." You know, "and stuff"! Then they asked, "Well, what do you think about Mrs. Boggess being in a wheelchair?" He looked at me like—Oh, she *is* in a wheelchair, isn't she! He said, "You know, that's kinda sad, isn't it."

I'm in constant pain. I have back pain and especially pain in my feet and legs—they're on fire. Burning all the time. The closest analogy I can come to is when your circulation is cut off and your feet, your hands or whatever, are asleep. It's the pins-and-needles sensation—all the time. When I'm very, very tired, it gets to me. I try not to take any medication. There are times I have to, for pain. Most of the time, if I get adequate rest, I'm okay. But my regular day would put a lot of people in an emergency room.

My alarm goes off at 5:30, and I get up. Obviously it takes me longer to take my shower, do my hair and makeup, then lie on the bed and get dressed. I have to roll back and forth to get my slacks on; I wear thigh-high hose now, instead of panty hose. After I get dressed, I'm in my chair and starting breakfast and getting my children up by quarter after six. They're efficient. They get themselves dressed. They get their own cereal out.

Then it's a collective effort. My son takes the keys out to the van, starts the van, warms it up for us. They go out, let out the lift so that, when we leave, I roll onto the ramp—onto my little wheelchair lift. It raises me up. They're in the van waiting; I swing in, transfer into the driver's seat, and since I'm going that way anyway, I take them to school every day. They don't have to ride the school bus.

They're just great. They're a lot of help. Of course, they have their days—"Mom, nobody else has to do this. Why do I have to do this?" I say, "I did this when I was a kid. I cleaned my room. I had my jobs. And you're going to do the same thing."

I get to school. I have to be in my room by 8:00. I get my things prepared for the day. My lesson plans are prepared by the week. My first class is at 8:30 every day, and each class has between seventeen and twenty-three students. First grade through sixth grade—six to thirteen, fourteen years old. I'm in an inner-city situation. They're wonderful, though. I wouldn't trade it for anything right now. It's kind of hard sometimes. I have to leave it at school because some of their situations are so heartbreaking. A little girl I had last year—a thirteen-year-old sixth grader—had a baby this summer. The man who fathered the child came at the beginning of school. I don't know what exactly happened, but she ended up killing this man. She and her mom—her mother helped her—they stabbed him to death. The man was thirty-three. This type of thing just tears your heart out. But these things happen to my kids. I have several children—boys and girls—who have been sexually abused and are in counseling. I have several children who are physically abused on a regular basis. One little fellow's mom came to school demanding to know what we had told the social workers. "What'd you tell them!" Just stormed right into the classroom without any permission. She hadn't been home for days. The boy had been beaten, horribly. A little black boy—I mean the bruises and the marks on his body! It was just so obvious what had happened. Of course, the authorities are taking steps to see if they can't do something—get the mother in a program or remove the boy from the situation so he's not subjected to this. All that day, that little boy wanted to go home—"I want to go see how my mom is. She's upset." He still wants to take care of her, even though she's abusing him so horribly.

It's awful! It's real sad. But you have to deal with it. You know, the words that come out of their mouths—you can't make a big deal out of it. If they came out of my child's mouth, I'd get very upset. But so many of them see Mom hit the streets at night— that's how they make money. They witness all kinds of things, in the home, coming in and out. A little girl performed oral sex on a little boy on the playground last year in front of everybody. It was on a dare.

Let me tell you about Anthony. Anthony was my fourteen-year-old sixth-grader last year. He'd walk down the hall and talk, and you'd think a man was there. I mean, he was five foot ten or eleven, hundred forty, fifty pounds—big guy—deep voice—the only other man, other than our principal and gym teacher, in the school. Anthony was not real academically inclined to say the least. He's going to be a football player somewhere. In my classroom, one particular student was giving him a real hard time. She wouldn't leave him alone. So, behind my back, Anthony gave her the finger, and the whole class cracked up. I knew something had happened. The little boy beside me whispered: "Ms. Boggess! Anthony just gave Pam the finger!" "Okay, thanks, Chris." So I turned around and I said, "Anthony, what's the problem?"

"Nothing, Mrs. Boggess. Not a thing."

He can be so polite and nice when he needs to be. I said, "Well, what's this?" showing him my finger. His eyes got real big. I could see it going through his mind—"My God, I'm going to get kicked out in the first week of school." He said, "I don't know. What is it?"

"Nothing," I said. "I'll tell you what I'm going to do, Anthony. I'm going to pretend that this was a map of West Virginia . . . and that you were showing Pam where Huntington was on the map of West Virginia. And that you will never perform this gesture in my classroom again. Nothing will be said, and you won't go to the office, and you'll be a very nice, polite young man, and we won't have any more of this at all in my room."

"No problem, Ms. Boggess. I understand."

You've got to laugh a lot of times, rather than cry. You've just got to say, "Oh, gosh!" The day I got my new motorized wheelchair, I decided to go show it to the neighbors. So I cut through the yard, going to show it to my girlfriend on the next street over. I was so proud of this machine; it was so neat that I was going to be able to do so many more things without getting tired. And I hit a pothole—the front tire went down in the pothole, and I flew out of the chair and broke my leg!

"Oh, my God!" I rolled over. My little girl was walking down the street to her friend's house. No one else in sight on the street. I yelled, "Jenny, go get Kathy and Jeff." By the time they all got to me, I had rolled over and I was lying there as if I was getting some sun or something. Jeff said, "My God, Pam—what a way to get attention!"

I'm thinking about getting married again. He's a real cutie. I'm scared to death. He's my best friend Shernie's little brother. She said, "D.J.'s coming home. I can't wait for you to meet him. You're going to fall in love with him." She didn't know. "You guys will really have a good time together. He's a musician. He's very creative in his own right. And very energetic. Mr. Personality." And I thought, "Great! I can't wait to meet this guy." I didn't know how old he was or what he was going to look like. I'd never seen any pictures. I had no idea what I was getting into.

The first time I saw him he was this little, short fellow with a baseball cap on. He looked in the window of my van and he said, "Hello, Pam. How are you." I said, "Fine. It's nice to finally meet you." I was kind of disappointed. I wasn't at all impressed. Then he sort of started showing up everywhere. Everyplace we would go, there was Shernie's little brother. He would clean up a little better every time, it seemed like. He started looking better and better. So we'll see.

I talk with people. I go to hospitals and talk to people who have just become paraplegics and are just starting what I've already been through. I'm sort of a pseudocounselor. I don't have a counseling degree, but they can talk to me and ask me anything they want. And I will talk to them about any questions they might have—their fears.

Religion gave me strength. Religion gave me something to look forward to. I don't have to concentrate on my limitations here because there are unlimited possibilities once I die and am in heaven. Because I really believe that there is a place that we will go. And the promise of this other life—I'll be just like everybody else there. I won't be in a wheelchair there.

Virginia Spurlock:

In the spring of 1989, Pamela Boggess's mother sent the following message: Pam told her doctor at Vanderbilt that she had lived more in this last seven years of her life than most people do in a lifetime.

For all her disabilities, she did a lot of artwork. She told me once that, if it hadn't been for her art, she didn't know what she would have done after she became paralyzed.

She said to me one day, "Mom, I'm dying, and I hate it. There's so many things I wanted to do." We did everything we knew to do for her, and there just wasn't anything else. After she saw her children the last time, she never talked to us anymore. She lost her eyesight, and then she just went into a coma and passed away on May 10, 1989.

■
CHUCK CLOSE

A well-known art critic suggested I talk to
Chuck Close, describing him as one of the best
artists in the U.S. today despite a crippling illness that could well have halted him in mid-
career.

Born in Monroe, Washington, Close at-
tended the University of Washington, doing
postgraduate work at Yale University's School
of Art and Architecture. His work, which in the
main consisted of large-scale black-and-white
paintings, was shown in 1969 at the Whitney
Museum of American Art. Since then, countless
individual and group exhibitions, as well as
articles, catalog essays, and books on contemporary art have increased his reputation. In
1992 he was elected a member of the American
Academy and Institute of Arts and Letters.

I interviewed him in his studio in Greenwich
Village. He greeted me with warmth and enthusiasm. He was very frank with me. He said he
could get out of his wheelchair and stand for
only a few minutes; he showed me how with his
mouth he puts his paintbrush into a device

strapped to his wrist. Without a shred of self-
pity he shared some of the problems that
impeded his recovery from a completely un-
foreseen and near-fatal illness.

Born near Seattle, I grew up out there for the first twenty-one years of my life. I came East to go to graduate school at Yale. I wanted to be an artist when I was probably three or four. My parents were rather supportive of the idea . . . a better one, more interesting, certainly, than becoming a doctor or lawyer or whatever. My mother had been a classically trained pianist, but the Depression had come along and she never performed: She taught piano. My father was sort of itinerant, a jack-of-all-trades.

From the first, I had a lot of learning disabilities. I really didn't know what they were until recently, because in the forties and fifties no one I knew had ever heard of dyslexia or other learning disabilities. I was seen as a shirker, lazy or dumb. So I had a lot of trouble. I read very slowly with very little comprehension. I had an almost total inability to memorize anything and spit it back. I even had difficulty in recognizing faces, which may have inadvertently pushed me in the direction I'm working today—trying to scrutinize the faces of the people I know and love, and trying to figure out what they look like.

Even though I seemed to be a failure on many levels—the school didn't think I was doing very well, I couldn't do very well on the ball field, and so on—I always did feel special, and I think that my parents helped to instill that. I felt special because I had discovered that I could make art, and that was something my friends couldn't do. So I put all my eggs in that basket. You know, there's a tremendous advantage to narrowness. Many people are talented in so many areas that they have a difficult time focusing; their life is very scattered. They do this for a while and that for a while, and they spin their wheels in the sand, endlessly trying to figure out what it is they want to do with their lives.

For me there was never any question. Art was the only thing I could do and that was that; so I'd better be good at it. This may have helped me when I got sick, because the desire to get back to work was strong. It was like, "Well, this is the only thing I can do. I've got to figure out how to paint again."

Anyway, when I got into college, despite my learning disabilities, I realized I could find my own way to skin a cat—by doing work for extra credit, different kinds of projects, and figuring out in which classes I would be able to be successful. Rather than taking courses requiring writing in-class essays, I picked classes in which I could write a paper and then have someone else correct the spelling and type it.

So in a way the system—though it seemed stacked against me—probably stood me in good stead when it came to the more recent problems I've had since I became a quadriplegic.

I was at Gracie Mansion in New York giving an award to someone. I suddenly had a tremendous pain in my chest that went through my back and my arms. I thought it was a heart attack. I went across the street to Doctors Hospital where, within a very short time, I was totally paralyzed from the neck down. It was several days before they figured out what had happened, which was that an occluded or collapsed spinal artery had cut off the flow of blood to my spine and knocked out nerves all over my body. Virtually everything from the shoulders down was affected. I was totally paralyzed to begin with; then, for a year and a half until it stopped, I got some "return." But all my muscles are compromised to one degree or another, some more than others. I can move my arms. My hands don't work at all. For an artist, the two great fears are your eyes and your hands.

I was frightened, but I'll tell you, there's something very calm about it too. It's like being in a car accident—at the exact moment the car is spinning out of control and about to careen into an oncoming bus or whatever, there's a sense of calm when you're actually going through it. Then, once you know you've survived, you shake; you fall apart and kind of go into shock.

I found that to be the case while I was in intensive care in a real life-threatening situation. I was on a lot of drugs, steroids—things really playing havoc with my brain. I was hallucinating. So I don't know how frightened I was. But my recollection was that it was quite calm and not as scary as when the deadening reality of the kind of day-in and day-out existence of not being able to move really set in. On the tenth, eleventh, twelfth day you haven't moved a muscle from your shoulders on down, and people are rolling you over and back and attaching tubes and things, *that's* when you think, "Oh, it's never going to get any better than this." That's when it really gets scary.

I was mentioning before that it's hard to imagine how you can make art without your hands—it's so hard to create art anyhow. But it's possible. If you already know how to make art and something like this happens to you, you can figure out how to get back to it. When I was in the hospital someone said to me, "Oh, you'll be okay. You paint with your head and not with your hands." I thought to myself at the time, "Easy for you to say," and it sort of made me angry. But the person, whoever it was, was absolutely right. I mean, once you know what art looks like, you can figure out some way to push the stuff around until you get it to look like art.

I remember lying there in bed when I was paralyzed and thinking, "Well, now what will I do?" So I thought, "I'll make work of a more conceptual nature. I'll get someone else to execute it." Then, when I got a little more head-and-shoulder movement, I thought, "Well, I can paint with a brush in my teeth, or I'll spit the paint on the canvas. I'll do something!" Finally, I began to get enough arm movement to figure out ways to get back to work. Surreptitiously my wife had spoken to the occupational therapist and said, "We've got to find a way to get Chuck back to work." She encouraged the occupational therapy department to build me a wheelchair-accessible easel and to adapt orthotic devices to hold a brush. At first, I had some help; someone stood next to me and helped me get the brushes in and out of a brush holder. Now I do that with my teeth. I made the first of the paintings that I'll be showing this year, three years later.

Throughout all this, I had some good therapists, some not-so-good therapists, some good doctors, and some terrible doctors. I had one doctor who was supposed to be monitoring my entire program—physical therapy, occupational therapy, and so on. He never once came to see me in the therapy rooms. Never, ever saw me move a muscle so he could make decisions about what kind of therapy I should get. Kept me from electromuscular stimulation until my muscles were all wasted away.

Hospitals can be incredibly dehumanizing. A rehab hospital—in this case Rusk—is a very unusual kind of society. It has its own structure, its own crazy, wacky rules; you learn to live within it. If you try to beat the system, it can be very demoralizing and embarrassing . . . it is humiliating to be left in your own feces for hours. Even the choice to fight is interesting. You can try and get what you want by being—well, I tried to be especially nice, figuring that people would be more likely to give me what I needed if they liked me. Those people who fought harder for what they wanted—and were absolutely justified—often didn't get a thing. Being nice paid off better.

My occupational therapist likes to tell this story, so I think I can tell it. She wanted me to do my laundry, so we rolled down the hall to where the washers and dryers were. At that point I was really in much worse shape than I am now; I couldn't lean over at all. I struggled to get the damn washing machine open to put stuff in. Then later we had to come back and get it out and put it in the dryer. I had to use a stick with a hook to get the stuff out because I couldn't lean over to get at it. It just took an inordinate amount of time, like hours, to do a little bit of laundry.

So it became clear to her right away that I had such a limited amount of energy that I'd be better off painting and not trying to do the laundry. I was going to be a much more cheerful person if I were painting and hell to be around if I was doing laundry.

I remember one day she tried to get me to type. To do this I had a pencil stuck in a brace, so I had to hit one key at a time. I said to her in the middle of this: "Listen, I never typed a letter before I came in the hospital. Why should I start now? I always had somebody who typed letters for me before, and after I get out I'll have them type them then."

So she realized right away that what she needed to do was help me get back to those things that I had prioritized, that were important to get back to. And doing laundry and typing wasn't.

I spent seven months in the hospital. I watched the patients and finally concluded that they were either optimistic or pessimistic. That was it. It's really almost genetic—the predisposition toward one or the other is so great. So I found it very difficult to be judgmental of people who gave up, because they were doing the best they could. They just weren't equipped. They didn't have the reservoir of optimism or whatever that other people quite naturally seem to have. It didn't have anything to do with how bad off they were or how severe a hand they were dealt. Some people were dealt very severe hands and were able to play them quite nicely. Other people just weren't. It almost seems like something you can't take any credit for or really have any control over. Some people have an ability to summon up that kind of will very easily—tap it and get to it with relative ease. Other people, with all the encouragement in the world—loving supportive families, great therapists—just aren't able to get up for it.

There's a blame-the-victim aspect of this, too. Something awful has happened to you but, if you don't have the right attitude, it's like there's something wrong with you personally. I think a good attitude and everything is great if you've got it, but it's very hard to manufacture it if you don't.

I thought that if I had a good attitude and worked really hard—I'm someone who's used to being an achiever—I'd overcome problems. So I went into this program and I thought, "Get out of my way. I'm really going to set this place on fire. I'm going to be the hardest-working patient they've ever had. I'm going to have the best attitude." I never skipped a therapy session. I never cut out early. But then I would see someone next to me with the worst attitude in the world—wouldn't go, didn't care, whined, sat in the corner. And they got better and walked out of the place. And I didn't get better and I was stuck there. Then I realized that your body gets better when your body wants to get better, and it doesn't when it doesn't. Attitude doesn't make up for everything. And working hard doesn't make up for everything. And you cannot just will yourself where you want to go.

One of the things that I found in the hospital was that, if it isn't based in reality, there's something sort of artificial about encouragement . . . as if a bubbly attitude is going to be infectious and sweep the other person along, out of funk and out of doldrums, out of feeling sorry for themselves. And we're all hearing, "Aren't we going to have a wonderful experience pushing the marbles around today."

So part of it is being able to learn to accept the hand that was dealt you and then figure out how best to play it. You cannot play it the same way someone else would.

Those people with faith, I think, find it very sustaining and very helpful. I was raised in a church, but I don't have a personal faith. At one point I felt I might die. But I wasn't one of those people in the foxholes who had a little last-minute conversion. I had people praying for me. I had friends on the West Coast who sent me crystals to rub on my body. Even some people who believe in charismatic faith-healing and things like that were working on me. But I myself didn't have that to fall back on.

For me, one of the things is that, as an optimistic person, I'm used to looking for light at the end of the tunnel. At first, my optimism gave me hope that I would continue to get more return, continue to get better. Finally, when reality sets in, when you realize you are not going to get anything more, then it's tough. We all age. As the aging process sets in, everybody finds movement and things increasingly difficult; if every muscle in your body is already compromised, then you have to look forward to a life of deterioration from an already disadvantaged position.

It's interesting to watch stroke victims. They can look terrible, I mean, look like they're never going to do anything again—just sitting in a wheelchair drooling. They can't recognize anybody. They can't walk. They can't do anything. But there isn't a brain that can't regenerate. Within a matter of months these people are often walking out of the place, looking terrific, ready to go back to a relatively normal life. Someone else—especially someone with spinal cord injuries, there are no nerves in the spine to regenerate—is knocked out. So attitude in that case is not going to make the difference. Life is unfair. If somebody with a bad attitude gets better and somebody with a good attitude doesn't, what are you going to do?

When you're in the hospital as a quadriplegic, it's very funny:
You don't envy regular people. You envy paraplegics. If only the
upper half worked, then everything would be all right. I remember when I was a kid I couldn't run and I couldn't hit a ball. I
would fantasize that I would be a great player, but since I really
couldn't run—I mean, I couldn't get fifty feet without falling
down—I would fantasize that I was a great baseball player because if I could hit a home run every time, it meant I could almost
walk around the bases. I accepted part of my limitation in order
to fantasize about the rest of it. I found a way to deal with not
being able to run. And in a way that's what life is like when you've
been dealt a blow like this. You say, "Okay. What happened?
Now, if I don't get anything more back, what will I do? If I do get
more back, great. That will be the extra added bonus. But if I
don't, how can I start operating at this level? At least I'm preparing for this—for what's real, for what's do-able." So that was sort
of the approach that I took, and I think that's pretty much what
the therapists were doing.

When I was lying in the bed in the hospital the art world really
came out. I mean, really supported me. Many people came to my
bedside every day. I had so many visitors I felt sorry for people
around me who were not visited very often. Every day, every
night, I would look over the end of my feet at the foot of my bed
at the face of another art-world person or friend or family member looming there in the dark . . . this sort of disembodied face.
It really brought home to me just how important these images are.

One of the things that became clear to me early on was how
important it was to have something to do, something that you're
anxious to get back to. I wanted to get back to work because I
enjoy what I do. I love making art. I wanted to get back to work
because, besides being a husband and father, it's largely how I see
myself. I'm an artist—therefore I have to make art. I had to get
back to work and prove that I'm an artist.

Also, and this is very important as well, I had to support my
family. I wanted to get back to work to pay the bills. But in the
seven months I was in the hospital, and another year that I was
an outpatient going there almost daily, I noticed very few people

were anxious to get back to work. I think this ultimately is sort of an indictment of what's happening in our society: Jobs are so boring or dead-end or not stimulating or whatever, so that given half a chance, people would choose *not* to go back to work. I think they are finally cheating themselves of the value of work, because I know the days I don't work move by at glacial speed . . . so long, long, depressing, and hard. Those days when I go to the studio to work fly by.

So getting someone back to work should be the goal of therapy. A lot of people I met were paraplegics, so the upper half of their bodies were fine. No reason why they couldn't sit at a desk and use a computer or do any kind of office jobs. It's funny: When I went to occupational therapy, I said to the therapist, "Help me with my occupation." I thought that's what it meant. But that isn't what "occupational therapy" really means. It means to keep you occupied. You sit around and you stack up spools and tie laces and stuff like that, which are activities that are very important because it's good for you to move your muscles, your arms, and to get someone back doing something. And it's geared toward independence at home, independence in living . . . being able to open the refrigerator and take care of yourself a little bit. But very, very little of it is geared to help patients regain the skills necessary, either to get back to the original work they were doing or, failing that—if that is going to be impossible—some kind of alternative training to do some other kind of activity.

I think it's important that the particular solutions I've found are applicable to my life; I was able to fashion them, to make them work. But they're not necessarily hints that I can give to someone else, and then be annoyed if they don't seem to work the same way they do for me.

Who would guess that I would be able to get back to painting? Your hands don't move and your arms don't work the way they used to work. You can't walk around and stand up. But actually, my art is the most normal aspect of my life. It's the thing that's changed the least. Because I could get help, get equipment, have devices made and thus alter my working conditions enough to have a great deal of control over my environment and my workplace. I really was able to get back to something close to a normal work life.

Of course, some things have changed. I miss most, I guess, the solitude. One of the reasons I became an artist was to be able to go into a room by myself and be alone. That, unfortunately, has pretty well gone by the wayside, since I do need help every once in a while and I have to have people around. I'm a very social person. I love being with people, but I've always enjoyed going into the studio and doing my work alone. I have difficulty concentrating sometimes, which I think is partially due to my learning disabilities, and if I'm distracted by other people being in the room, it's a little harder to focus.

I'm sure there are things that I used to do that I couldn't do today. It just so happens that what I was doing at the time this happened was something I was able to get back to without a great deal of difficulty. I'm luckier than a lot of quads in that I can stand up. I can take a few steps. I use quad-crutches that strap to my arms. I can't walk very far, not enough to really be practical, but, believe me, it's easier to get up a couple of steps into a building than being stuck in a wheelchair 100 percent of the time and having to be dragged up the steps. As for painting, I have an orthotic device that straps with Velcro around the middle of my forearm, around my wrist and my fingers and thumb. If I move my wrist in a certain way, I can get a little sort of involuntary grip—enough to get a brush out of a brush holder. To work on the tops of paintings I have a forklift truck that takes me up in the air, actually something that I used when I wasn't handicapped. It allows me to spend hours up at the top of my painting, which is usually about nine feet high.

Actually all my work for the last twenty-five years or so has been built out of little pieces—out of incremental parts. It's a way of thinking that may be an outgrowth of my learning disabilities. When things seem too big to deal with you break them down into a lot of bite-size pieces. Working incrementally is more akin perhaps to the problems of a writer. My paintings often take twelve or fourteen months, which is more the kind of time span, of energy and attitude, that someone writing a long piece or a novel would try to sustain. Just as a writer fashions a complex thought word by word, slamming one word into another, by building, fashioning a thought out of trying this word and then another to see how they affect each other, that's what I try to do with paint. I try to put strokes next to each other and see how they influence the way the strokes around them read. I start at the top of a canvas and I work to the bottom, trying to remember what it felt like to make the first piece, the way a writer has to remember what it felt like to write the first chapter so it still seems like the same person is writing it at the end.

To use another analogy: If you think of an architect, there's nothing about the brick an architect is going to use that says anything about the kind of building that's going to be built. If you stack up the bricks one way, you build a cathedral; if you stack them up another way, you make a gas station. I'm very interested in using marks—my fingerprints—strokes of paint, little gobs of pastel, little pieces of paper pulp—because there's nothing about the incremental mark itself which predetermines its use. It's only the way they go together that builds something into a coherent image, something you'd recognize and that has meaning.

After I got back to work, I didn't want all of a sudden to become known as the "handicapped artist." People around me were very reluctant at first to let me do interviews; they were very protective of me. I'd had a successful fifteen-, twenty-year-long career as an artist. Now all of a sudden not to be seen as an artist anymore, but as a "handicapped" artist, was a risk. Would people think differently about what I made? So that was a real fear. It was very important that the very first large painting I made when I got out of the hospital was bought by the Museum of Modern Art . . . not only important for me, but important to the art world, because it was sort of a Good Housekeeping seal of approval. The Museum of Modern Art is not in the business of buying handicapped art, you know, just to make someone feel better.

There's a new urgency to what I do. It does mean more to me. I don't have other things in my life competing for my attention and interests as much. There's just my work and my family.

I have an older daughter who's in college. She's nineteen. And

I have a seven-year-old daughter. The contrast between what I was able to do with my older daughter and what I'm now able to do with my younger one is very upsetting; I think it's upsetting for her as well. She feels cheated, no question, and I do too. I would love to get down in the grass and roughhouse with her and pick her up and carry her around. This has been extremely devastating on the family. This is not something that just happens to the victims, to the patient or whoever. In many ways it's much harder to watch something happen to someone you love than to have it happen to yourself. Everyone asks how *I* am. No one asks how my wife is. Her life has changed in many ways, almost more than mine. She's a young woman, and a lot of things that we did together we can't do. She's facing a lifetime of us not being able to do the things we always did and enjoyed. It's like the rings from a pebble in a pond—they just keep getting wider and wider, until they seem to affect everyone who comes in contact with them. It's hard for the kids. If I visit my daughter at school or camp, she has to explain to everybody why I'm in a wheelchair. I can't just be a daddy visiting at school. The focus is not on me going there to see her schoolwork or her artwork or whatever. It ends up being on how I am going to get into the school. It's a big entrance when I come into a room in a wheelchair; it's often difficult for a young child to always have to explain. I think she'd like a more normal life.

As for me, I'm very uncomfortable. Physically, I have sensations, but I don't have regular-type sensations. It feels like my hands are in ice water. There are all kinds of strange things like that that are annoying. Though I'm not really in pain, my rear end hurts from sitting all day. I have nearly constant bladder infections. I'm always on antibiotics and other things that are debilitating, demoralizing, and painful.

I still go to the theater, but I run the risk of looking down and seeing that I have a lap full of urine. You can decide that you're going to stay home where nobody will see this, where no one will know that you've had an accident. Or you can decide to go out anyway, even though such things can happen. It takes its toll!

Really, what I miss most is walking on the beach. I love the ocean and I love swimming. I can float in a pool. I have a regular pool in the country, which I walk in. But I miss nature, because I used to love being outdoors. There are a few wheelchair-accessible state parks that I'm looking into . . . where there are wooden paths instead of trails. I don't mind being pushed through the streets. I'm not self-conscious about it. Some people find that very difficult; they don't go out because they feel everyone is staring at them; they just find it too difficult. They would rather stay home. I would rather get out and see what's going on in the world.

Of course, the fact is that I don't ever see very many people like me in the street, especially in Soho, where everything is inaccessible. There are no curb cuts. Everything is up two or three steps. And even uptown, where I live on the Upper West Side, there are very few curb cuts and things are difficult. It is really incredible to me how little effort has been made to make this society accessible to people with handicaps. It's something, of course, that I didn't notice very much before, though I'm acutely aware of it now.

I've called to get handicapped tickets for Carnegie Hall and arrived to find that the seat was down ten steps and five places in. I'd like to know how they think *that's* accessible.* I go with assistants and other people who could help me get in there, but for somebody simply going by themselves—well, they would have had to turn around and go back home.

If they're accessible, some movie theaters are better. But I've called theaters and asked if they're accessible; they'll say yes, which turns out to mean you can open the front door and go in, but once inside you have to go up a flight of stairs to the theater from the lobby. I mean, what do they think I came in to do—buy popcorn? It makes me wonder.

In the evenings, we'll get a car service or a driver, especially if

---

*Carnegie Hall was remodeled in 1988 and is now accessible. There is an accessible entrance on Fifty-seventh Street. There is a manned elevator—it also has lowered floor buttons and raised lettering for the visually impaired—which makes all levels accessible. There is wheelchair seating on the parquet level (orchestra seating). They do recommend that persons with special requirements call ahead and inform the box office.

my wife is dressed up. I mean, for her to pick up a muddy wheelchair in the rain and throw it in the back of the van when she's dressed for the opera is not very sensible. I'm actually going to take a course in driving (I would have to get a van modified), but the problem is that it's almost impossible to use one in the city. In the suburbs there are large parking lots and spaces for the handicapped, but there is no handicapped parking in New York City . . . not a single handicapped parking space in the entire city!* It's not as hard in the country, although, strangely, I find being in the country harder emotionally because I can't control my environment. In the city, I have things set up at home, in the studio, and I have help to get from one to the other . . . places I go for lunch and other things that I know how to do. In the country I find myself sitting on our deck watching other people mow the lawn and dig in the garden and do all the things that I used to do and loved doing so much.

The fact is the world is pretty hostile to people with handicaps. I'm not angry at the world. But there's a lot that should be done. I am not an activist. Some people I've met have made this their life's work—to fight to get greater access and other things for the handicapped. I'm glad they're there. I try to do a certain amount of that. I try to give interviews or speak or work with organizations. But I've only so much energy. Basically I felt that the best thing I could do was to get back to work. I mean, I'm not trying to be a role model for anybody. I don't believe I'm a hero. This is just survival. This isn't heroic. This is just trying to get through every day, trying to make sure that there's some pleasure every day.

Mainstreaming people who can't really function is a cruel thing to do if all it does is to call into question how they *can't* do it . . . especially if they're battering their head against the wall day in and day out and never succeeded in anything. Mainstreaming has to fit the needs of the individual very carefully. This is some-

*The New York Department of Motor Vehicles will issue a permit to persons with disabilities that allows them to park in "handicapped" spaces any car displaying this permit. Special license plates can be obtained for a car registered to a "handicapped" person.

thing that hospitals and rehabilitation programs are starting to address, but I don't think they're doing it as well as a lot of other things. They either make the same goal for everybody, which means that some people fall miserably short and feel like failures, or they lower everything to the ground, expecting that you'll never be able to do anything anyway . . . and that suggests we should all go in a room and, you know, bounce a ball to each other. There seems to be almost nothing in between . . . just a big gray area.

I have a lot of trouble with all these names. You know what I hate? "Physically challenged." Everybody who went through rehabilitation with me hated things like that. We all called ourselves gimps. I mean, there was something about *accepting* what happened. I understand why society at large and in general does not want to refer to someone in any way which is demeaning or degrading. You don't want to call somebody a cripple, because it seems derogatory. But it's important for the person to accept words like "cripple" and not have it sting. That's why there's a lot of self-mocking, like using "gimp."

So, you have to look at whether the person is reentering society on the same level with nonhandicapped people. If the person can equip himself or herself, and if society can help, along with hospitals and other places, the ideal would be to have that person reenter without a label. That does not mean they have to have advantages. Just access to get through the door. And maybe a bathroom that they can get into. Hopefully, they can do the same job anybody else can, and pretty soon their handicap becomes invisible.

So I want to have my paintings judged with the best paintings being made by anybody. Not just people who are handicapped. That was why I wanted to reenter the regular art world and to be seen just as an artist.

■

GEORGE COVINGTON

George Covington is Special Assistant for Disability Policy in the office of the vice president. He answers all the letters pertaining to disability issues, many by telephoning people directly. He recently wrote a book entitled Crippling Images, *which deals with fighting the myths and negative images and stereotypes of people with disabilities. He will continue in this work because he "wants to do something interesting that will make a difference." He feels strongly that people with disabilities should be treated no differently from anyone else, and that opportunities should be open to them. "Some of us with disabilities are charming, witty, and highly intelligent; some of us are not. The disability didn't determine which of us would be sexy and which of us would be sexist. A disability gives us a different perspective, not a different personality." One of his firm beliefs is that "we are people, and need to laugh." He wants all the barriers down so that "we can have a level playing field." He likes Very Special Arts because it means arts for all. A gregari-*

ous man with a beautiful wife (whose picture
he showed me) and a keen sense of humor, he
obviously enjoys what he is doing. He will most
certainly make himself heard in whatever field
he chooses.

I was born into a poor family in East Texas—poor but proud. I was born legally blind, with approximately 20–400 vision. It took a few years before my parents realized I had some type of visual problem. I had always been able to fake intelligence, so they really didn't know how bad it was until I got to school and had to walk up to the blackboard. The family ophthalmologist said it was a combination of what we've come to know as astigmatism, nystagmus, eccentric fixation, and myopia—all of which were acute—and probably even further back, a degenerating retina. There was no way of knowing then. I had that type of vision all the way through grade school. And I was a disciplinary problem as well. I thought I knew as much as the teacher—and I probably did. The school was called Grim Elementary, something Charles Dickens would not have touched. It *was* grim. My first-grade teacher was named Mrs. Steele. She gave me a paddling the first day of first grade. I was kept after school every day for talking. I lived at that time with my grandmother, who thought school let out an hour later than it did because I got home an hour later than everybody else.

The school didn't allow for even moderately bright children. I found most of my peers extremely dull, though fun to play with. I felt the school was confining. One day Mrs. Steele called me up to the front of the class and said, "George, if you have something to say, say it in front of the whole class." She was doing it as a disciplinary measure. I saw it as a wonderful opportunity. About an hour and a half later, she discovered she had made a really big mistake: I just rambled on and on and on, telling stories and so forth.

From the first grade, the authorities kept saying, "Send him to the school for the blind." But they were saying that because I was a disciplinary problem, not because I couldn't see. They were afraid, if they failed me, they'd have me in their class again. So they promoted me.

I was always described in school as "the little half-blind kid"— "the *mean* little half-blind kid." I wasn't mean, except that I talked. I just chattered constantly. When the teacher would make some statement, I would make a funny joke, and the class would laugh. I should have been a stand-up comic.

Actually, Mrs. Steele, when things got really tough, would call me to the front of the class and say, "Tell them a story." Then she'd leave the room. I would talk until she came back. Sometimes I wondered whether she went down and took a little nip to sort of fortify herself. Toward the end of first grade, she called me up to her desk and said, "Covington"—remember, she's talking to a six-year-old child—"Covington, if you ever earn an honest dollar in your life, it will be as a writer."

So I wasn't treated any differently from the others, really. That's probably one of the things that turned me into what I am today. I didn't know I was different. I played with kids. We'd jump over stuff, and I wouldn't jump clear because I didn't see the tops of the bushes. But there was never this "Oh, poor little blind kid." There was never "Oh, we have to make special arrangements for George." Nothing. In school, I walked up to the board, wrote down what I needed to, and walked back to my seat. That was it. They didn't know how to treat me, really. If I had been a passive blind kind, that would have been one thing. I was a very unpassive blind kid.

On the other hand, if I hadn't been so bright, and somewhat precocious, the system would have beaten me down. I'd probably be pumping gas in a small town in East Texas.

Of course, I just couldn't play baseball as well as everybody else. Several times I caught the softball coming down from a high fly right between the eyes. But Mother said if I could make the honor roll in school, she would buy me a baseball, a bat, and a glove. Well, I knew Mother and my stepfather could not afford to buy me any of those things. But I thought, what the hell—try for it. Since then, I never had another problem with grades. I made the honor roll. And Mother *was* able to buy me the baseball glove, which I was more than happy with—I didn't figure I'd get the bat and the ball anyway.

In those days I was always interested in art. I loved pretty things. We were poor, so what I did was collect glass. I'd go through the alleys and collect broken bottles, pieces of brightly colored glass: reds and blues and greens. To see them, I would hold the pieces up to the sun. I became a rock collector. I was very interested in being a "rockhound"—and there's not a lot of interest in rocks in East Texas, I assure you.

In class, I loved art. I was never encouraged. I accepted that. If they had said, "You can't do it," I would have done it just to spite them. But it didn't even reach the level of them saying, "You can't." It was simply an assumption that there was no way I could appreciate or enjoy art. It was so subtly done. That's the worst type of discrimination—the type that is so subtle that you're not aware of it, you are so low in their expectations that there's no way they would even *conceive* of you doing it. So they don't say anything, they don't *do* anything—that horrible assumption that if you're half blind, you couldn't have an aesthetic, you couldn't have an appreciation of beauty, you definitely could not produce anything that would be considered aesthetically pleasing. So my finger paintings were never exhibited, like the other kids'. Nobody was interested in my perspective. I was always drawing houses, rocket ships, rocket planes—living in my little fantasy world. I didn't have a lot of friends. I considered most other children my age to be absolutely stupid. I couldn't understand why they couldn't talk—carry on a decent conversation. In the first grade, I had the same language—the same verbal skills—as my parents and their peers. The Good Lord gave me a brain, and I used it.

By the time I was ten or eleven, I was spending my money on the Shreveport newspaper so that I could have something to read. It was the only thing I could afford. It was a dime. While the other kids were spending their ten cents on comic books, I bought the Shreveport newspaper because it was so much better than the Texarkana *Gazette*. To read, I used a high-powered magnifying glass.

When I was very small, six or seven, other kids were saying, "I want to grow up and be mayor," or "a cowboy." I said, "I want to grow up and be gone!" I didn't know if there was a world on the other side of the Texas and Pacific Southern tracks, which were on the other edge of town, but I sure the hell was going to find out. I didn't really realize what the world was like until I got to the University of Texas in 1964, on a Greyhound bus along with three cardboard boxes. I almost never went home again. I used to have to go home for Christmas, begrudgingly.

Mother always said, "Get as much of an education as you can." My mother taught me two things: One, education is important; and two, don't ever become a bigot. In East Texas, that was a difficult thing.

In my teen years, I was frustrated because I couldn't drive a car and pick up attractive young women and take them out to the park to do all the things in the back seat that everybody else was getting to do. But that was overcome when I got to the University of Texas; you didn't need a car for a date. I discovered nirvana. I discovered, too, that people didn't judge you by your old man owning a shoe store or used-car lots, which was the pinnacle of social achievement in Texarkana, Texas. When I got to the University of Texas and realized that it was just my brains against everybody else's, I thought it was going to be great. And it was. I spent ten years there getting a journalism degree, and a law degree, and enjoying myself. I wasn't really held back that much by poor eyesight.

One day I accidentally managed to run into one of the great educators in journalism, DeWitt C. Reddich. On this particular Saturday I was inspired to study for a change, so I ran over to the journalism school library; it was closed. As I was going down the hall, this elderly gentleman asked if he could help me. He said, "What are you looking for?" I said I was looking for a book by DeWitt C. Reddich on feature writing. He said he just happened to have that book in his office. I was too blind to see the name on the door when we went through it. A couple of weeks later, after I'd read the book, I returned it—and it was to DeWitt C. Reddich. He became my adviser and close friend. If it hadn't been for DeWitt C. Reddich, I would never have made it through journalism school. I didn't like the discipline of *any*thing. I didn't like self-discipline, I particularly didn't like authority. Journalism was a very undisciplined discipline, and it was perfect for me. What I discovered was that I had two choices: I could spend four hours reading what everyone else could read in thirty minutes, or I could read for thirty minutes, and then go spend three and a half hours at Shultz's Beer Garden. Which I did. I got by on minimal grades because I decided college was there to be enjoyed, and I was not going to waste it on academe.

I liked being a student. You weren't a bum if you were a student. I was in my early to mid-twenties at the time. I went on into law school. I thought a law degree would be good because it's like a plumber's license—nothing *but* a plumber's license. I don't have to practice law if I don't want to. I keep my law license. I give a lot of free advice in the legal area to friends.

To read in school I used the high-powered magnifying lens. Some of my books in law school I got on tape. I skimmed—which anyone will tell you that you can't do in law school. But I did. It's something I would not encourage other people to try—particularly when I later became a college professor. I discourage it in my own students.

While in law school, I met a beautiful woman. I've always been attracted to beautiful women, probably always will be as long as God makes them. She was a photographer, doing postgraduate work in photography. I'd always been fascinated with photography. I'd always wanted to do photography. But I knew I couldn't—it wasn't there for me to do. So I started carrying her equipment, which was heavy—forty, fifty pounds of equipment— around central Texas. Love and lust is one thing. But sitting for hours while she set up this camera made me wonder what I was doing out there in the middle of the wilderness. Then a strange thing happened. I would be working with her, setting up a scene. If you asked me what the scene was, I would tell you she was shooting a picture of a big boulder. When we'd get back to the darkroom and I'd help her with the processing, I would look at these 4″- × -5″ prints with my lens. I'd see that wasn't a rock at all. It was a tree stump! Or I would think she was photographing a bush. But in the picture, it turned out to be a rock. I suddenly realized I could see great detail in these 4″-×-5″ pictures that I couldn't see in the real world.

About the same time I discovered scale-focusing cameras in *Popular Photography*. Somebody wrote in to ask: "Do you need to see to focus a camera?" The answer was that scale-focusing is the oldest kind of focusing; it sets the camera. Two major cameras that had scale-focusing were available—one was a Rollei and one was a Petri. I sent off for catalogs, read about these cameras, and saw that there was a way I could use them. So I ordered myself a Rollei—a little 35-mm. scale-focusing camera—and started shooting pictures while my friend was out taking *her* pictures. I took over 3,000 photographs in two years, almost 2,000 of the woman. At the time she had a Volkswagen "Beetle." The lighting was perfect. I took hundreds of pictures of her driving—profiles. She kept looking over, and we nearly got run over a couple of times. But the lighting was perfect. I always set the camera on f3.5, I always had the shutter speed at a sixtieth of a second, and the distance at three feet. Perfect! The Volkswagen was like a little studio on wheels.

She thought it was great! She never really understood what kind of eyesight I had. Her theory was that if I could see the sun, which was ninety-three million miles away, I wasn't that blind. So, as a joke, she walked me into ditches and low branches and things like that. She was a very sweet-natured person, but she lacked a lot of common sense. A beautiful woman, highly intelligent—extraordinarily intelligent.

She encouraged me. I started learning and teaching myself darkroom techniques.

After I got the camera, I began doing portraits of people, primarily because I wanted to see faces above all. And I discovered something really strange. When I took pictures of old friends and processed and printed the film, their faces looked like I remembered them. But with new friends, I started seeing photographs of people I didn't know. I realized that my eyesight had closed down to a point where imagination had taken over. When I did self-portraits, I expected to find that I was a young Robert

Redford—and instead I found a young Groucho Marx! I've never really gotten over that one! I really was startled to find I didn't look like I thought I looked. I began to realize that I'd better do a lot of photographing quickly if I were going to see the faces of people I cared about, the places that I had been. So I started walking from my apartment to the center of campus, a distance of about a mile and a half, by different routes—and I would take photographs every ten feet. And burn a lot of film. I would get these prints, sit down at a table, and not recognize where I had been. I had been walking those routes for ten years! I saw street signs. I saw awnings on buildings I didn't know were there. I also discovered that if I'd been in a good mood that day, I'd see these flowers at the side of the road, and take their pictures. It turned out they were crumpled-up Dixie cups. If I was in a bad mood, I'd take pictures of garbage alongside the road, and it would turn out to be flowers! I started recognizing how my moods even determine what it is I see and don't see. Many millions of people who have this type of vision loss go down streets every day and don't see. About twelve million have a significant vision loss that can't be substantially corrected. Most of them don't consider themselves legally blind, because they're not. They just have a vision loss that is enough so that they're not really seeing what they think they're seeing.

About this time I accepted a teaching position at West Virginia University School of Journalism. The lady and I came East. I began to get more and more involved in photography. That summer she wanted to go to a photo workshop; I wanted to go to New England. So we compromised on the Maine Photographic Workshop, which was in its second summer. I met many great photographers—Elliot Erwitt, Arnold Newman, Eva Rubinstein, Judy Dater, Eugene Richards. They encouraged me, "You're doing something; keep doing it." I photographed these people photographing—taking pictures of Arnold Newman, Elliott Erwitt, great photographers, teaching other students. I started studying the history of photography. I realized that, since the daguerreotype, different people elicit different reactions with their cameras; they get different pictures. I heard about a Victorian lady around the turn of the century who went out West with a big camera to photograph and then came back and made prints to see where she had been.

About that time I started getting a great deal of publicity. Some of it came through the Maine photo workshop. Some of the photographic magazines began to pick up my stuff. No one had ever known that there was a visually impaired photographer.

The media blew it up too much. The headline was always "blind photographer" instead of visually impaired photographer. BLIND MAN DOES PHOTOS. BLIND MAN SEES WORLD THROUGH CAMERA'S LENS. At that time—the late seventies—everybody was really into gimmicks, like developing their film in water from the Rhine, developing it with vitamin C—everybody had a gimmick. So the blind photographer fit right in. A lot of young photographers began to resent the fact that I could generate this type of media—stories from UPI and AP and nearly every newspaper in the country. And I can't blame them. If you're starving to death and you know your art's better than that of the guy who doesn't see, then you can be resentful at seeing an article in *The Washington Post*. Friends were saying things like that I was the most-written-about photographer with the exception of Richard Avedon. Though I was getting this publicity, I really wasn't interested in selling my photographs. I've never been interested in that. I've always been interested in *seeing* them. That's why I use the phrase, "Most people see to photograph; I photograph to see."

I basically stayed away from the artistic community. One of the most honest reactions I ever got was from a young female photographer at a party who said, "What kind of photography do you do?" I said, "Well, I just do a lot of portraits. I'm legally blind, so I just photograph to see, really." She said, "What a great shtick! That's a great shtick!" I said, "Well, you know, that's probably the most honest reaction I've ever gotten, but it's true."

I like what I do, and I consider it to be an art. I've had people tell me, "Well, how do you take responsibility for your work? After all, you don't see what you're doing." I said, "That's true; I don't see what I'm doing. But I do it so I can see what I did. And if I don't take responsibility for it, I'm certain that, within a year or two, somebody else will."

After all, there are too many dumb people in photography who don't know what they're doing, why they're doing it, or anything. They're doing it because they are "artists." As long as they know where the drugstore is so they can have their film processed, they are artists. That wasn't the point for me. I don't do it to earn money. Elliott Erwitt once said he will always be an amateur photographer, because an amateur loves what he's doing. Since I love what I'm doing, I guess that would make me an amateur artist. If I had my druthers, I would photograph all the time. My eyesight is going quickly now, it's much less than it was. So I need the photography to see more than ever before.

I started with a Rollei 35D. That's a regular, full-frame 35 mm. It's got everything that a major camera has, except it looks like a toy. When I first started photographing, a lot of my friends were having children. I documented the first two or three years of several children. They weren't intimidated by this camera. To them it was just something that was there—that they saw around my neck, like a crucifix, because it was so small and I wore it all the time.

The camera is not auto-focus, it's manual. I would prefer to do the thinking for my camera, rather than have the camera do the thinking for me.

Right now you're sitting across the table from me. It's not a particularly wide table, but it's not narrow either—I would guess that you're approximately five feet from me. Because you're wearing a bright white blouse and you have dark hair, closely cropped, if you didn't open your mouth, I wouldn't know you were a woman. You could be a male or female, you could be black or white. I can't tell. Your complexion is darker than your blouse, but that's all I can tell. As a matter of fact, if you didn't move or make a statement, you could be a mannequin for all I know. A faceless mannequin. So, knowing that you're not, I take out of my pocket a small strobe—a very powerful strobe for short distances, it's not good for more than about ten feet. I've had this strobe for more than ten years and I know what its capabilities are. It's a fully manual strobe, very inexpensive—they don't make them anymore because it's too cheap. The camera is easy to set. I can do the shutter speed by clicks, and I know if I click it all in one direction, it's B - 30 - 60 - 125 - 250 - 500. Or the other way: 500 - 250 - 125 - 60 - 30 - B. The same thing with setting the aperture— it clicks. I can feel the clicks, so I know what aperture I'm going to get. For the distance, I have to take out my little magnifying lens and look on the barrel, and then set the distance. I've got it set here on six feet. If we were outdoors and I was not using a strobe, I'd take my little magnifying lens and look at the little CDS meter on top, and it would tell me exactly what I needed to set it at, and what range. I seldom need to use it. On a bright sunny day, I know, with the film that I'm using, what I need to set it at. And then I just start shooting. If we're outside, I can work around you in a circle or a semicircle. Generally, I try to work within three to four feet because I like to see the face. I like to shoot the environment. The environment helps me remember the person. If I get in close and I get a good portrait, then I've got the face. And then if I back up, I can get the person in their environment. Basically, it creates a memory—a gestalt—of that person.

All of this I taught myself. For me it was 90 percent self-taught, 10 percent instinct. The instinct came with the experimentation. If it doesn't work, you try something else.

I kept trying to find whether there was anything written on visual impairment and photography, and there wasn't. So I wrote a photography manual called *Let Your Camera Do the Seeing: The World's First Photography Guide for the Legally Blind*. It was simply trying to cut out all of the bullshit from photography. Most photography manuals are full of a lot of aesthetic bullshit. The first thing I discovered about photography teachers is to be very wary of the ones who say, "I'm not going to teach you my aesthetic, I'm just going to teach you photography." Because they *all* teach you their aesthetic. That's easy to understand; if they tell you to print everything on a number 3 or 4 grade of paper, and do it thus and such a way, it's the way *they* like it. I like my prints on a number 5, a really good black-white contrast, and I like them a little overexposed. That's the way I see it better. I don't tell my students to do that. I've tried to teach them: Don't do what people tell you to do; do what is best for you.

Most people are fascinated by what I do. One woman described my work as "happy Diane Arbus." I'm trying to figure that one out since, if you know Diane Arbus's work, there's nothing happy about it. There are two pictures that fascinate a lot of people. One of them is a picture of a kid on a rocking horse, outside on a patio. In a pane of glass behind the child, you can see the photographer and the father. The father is trying to coax the kid to do something, which is so typical. It's all captured in that one picture. I couldn't see myself in that pane of glass. I couldn't see the father. I could just barely see the kid in front of me.

The other picture is of a friend of mine in his hippie days, holding up an ice cream in Waterville, Maine. Behind him on this billboard is a poster of a child with its mouth open; there's a bite missing out of the ice-cream cone. I don't know what makes me take the picture at the instant I do. I don't know what makes me get the particular image that I get. I try not to pose people because, generally, they come across as cold and frosty. Arnold Newman said in one of his articles, "I don't know what Covington does, but he does it consistently; so it's not luck."

I think my work is more important—in that it demonstrates how photography can be used as an accessibility tool to art—than it is as art itself. If it makes it as art, fine. But I'm more interested in how photography can be used in a museum setting to make it more accessible to visually impaired people. How you can take objects that are small and make them large enough to see—or objects that are too large and make them small enough to see. Such as Rembrandt's *Night Watch*.

When I first started teaching the visually impaired, I said there was no real reason to teach blind people. But several blind women came to me and said, "Let us give you a couple of good reasons *why* we should be able to photograph: First, we'd like to take pictures of guys who ask us out so our girlfriends can tell us what they look like; second, if we're traveling, we'd like people to be able to describe the scenes where we were at the time, and keep those memories, and have people in the future ask us about it, describe the scenes and ask, 'What do you remember there?' " So I started saying, "Okay, fine." There's no problem teaching blind people to do photography.

It's odd. We hear all the time that if you're without one sense, your other senses are enhanced. Bullshit! Bullshit! I was once interviewed by a young woman doing a freelance article for *The Boston Globe*. She leaned over the table and said, "Well, you know, I've heard it's true that all blind people are really nice people." I said, "Dear, I know several blind people who would be in prison if they weren't blind. They've worked it for all they can." I said, "Probably the worst son of a bitch on the face of the earth that I know is a blind guy. But there is one myth—if you want to print this in *The Boston Globe*—that is true about blind and visually impaired people. We make the best *lovers*." I said that the next day at the Fine Arts Museum in Boston—we had a hundred people there, including a dozen little old ladies from a geriatric center, with their white and blue hair—and they got up and gave me a standing ovation!

So, no—I don't hear any better. I have sinus trouble sometimes. In Washington, D.C. (as you know from the coughing-wheezing-sneezing), your senses are dead anyway if you breathe. I may hear things and interpret them differently. But my hearing isn't any better. If I had been with Custer, the Indians would have had no trouble running over the 7th Cavalry at the Little Bighorn—they wouldn't have had to worry about my hearing or smelling their horses beforehand. So, no, the senses don't get any better.

Being visually impaired, though, makes me pay a lot of attention to people. I have a lot more tolerance for people who have differences that I don't understand. I have, I think, a better grasp of civil rights. I once said that, as a white southern male, I never thought I would have to worry about my civil rights. But as I wrote the 504 regs for the Department of the Interior—the Handicapped Civil Rights rights—I realized that there is a lot of discrimination against those with disabilities. At some point you're treated differently. I remember traveling with a woman, coming back from Palm Beach. We walked into this small airport at West Palm Beach and I asked, "When is the plane for Washington?" The agent said, "Well, it's on the monitor above my head, up there." I made the mistake of saying, "Well, I'm legally blind." She turned to the woman I was with and shouted, "Tell him it's four o'clock." I said, "Lady, I said I was legally blind, not deaf."

Another time, I was touring an art gallery that had an exhibit of tactile art for blind people. The person giving the tour didn't realize that I was legally blind. I asked, "How many blind people have come through here?" She said, "Well, you know, it's August; and they don't go outside a lot when it's hot."

The prejudices are there because they've been ingrained, generation after generation. I've worked for a dozen years to change the attitude of the media toward disabled people. I had a National Media Education Workshop here a couple of years ago, on the Hill, in which I brought in twenty-five outstanding college seniors from accredited schools of the Association for Educational Journalism who wanted to be reporters, and worked with them to change some of these myths and stereotypes. Because, at journalism school, they don't necessarily leave their prejudices at the front door. They take them with them. Then you see "confined to a wheelchair" in articles; you see "bound to a wheelchair." I told them repeatedly: If you're talking about "bound to a wheelchair," you'd better be talking about kinky sex.

Or the term "physically challenged." Many, many disabled people hate the term "physically or mentally challenged." Why in the hell should we be challenged? It isn't us causing the barriers. It isn't us constructing the buildings that are inaccessible.

I am legally blind. I will most likely always be. There is something coming down the pike that might end all that. They are working on a process for removing cells from one retina and replacing them in another. But I'm forty-six years old. I don't really spend a lot of time dreaming about what I'm going to do if I get 20/20 vision. I have no concept of what real eyesight is. I always joke that if I'd had 20/20 vision, I'd probably have been an international cat burglar.

If I had been born with 100 percent vision, perhaps I would have been Indiana Jones. I love archaeology. In grade school, junior high, and high school, I used to spend the summers at the library, because it was air-conditioned (we didn't have an air conditioner at home). I read every book on archaeology. I was fascinated. But I knew with my eyesight there was no way I could go traipsing through the jungle—I'd probably end up stepping on a vine that turned out to be a pit viper of some kind.

But then think about this: Monet's greatest works were painted after he developed double cataracts. It influenced his *Waterlilies* paintings. The astigmatism that Matisse had shows up very clearly in his work—bright, vivid colors, no sharp edges. Degas— the foggy prints—the pictures of the young ballerinas—again, cataracts. The handicap doesn't make us different, but it can give us a different perspective, and sometimes can produce beautiful results. If I had no disability, I'd still have the same sense of humor. I'd still have the same ability to communicate. The disability doesn't affect my personality. I would be a bastard with it or without it. But it does make me look at and perceive things differently, makes me able to develop techniques of communication.

Some good has probably come from what has happened to me. Considering the place and the situation I was born into, I could have turned out to be a really bright bigot. Being different, and always feeling out of place, I gained a perspective that let me view civil rights in an entirely different way. I can't say fate was particularly cruel to me. If I'd had 20/20 vision, I might have been killed in a motorcycle wreck at eighteen, or a car crash; a number of my friends from East Texas went that way. Who knows? But it's not something I speculate on. I was born this way; I am this way; and I will probably die this way.

The first thing is: Don't feel sorry for yourself. Get off your butt and get out and figure out a technique. High technology has produced a world full of things that'll cover almost any aspect of coping with a disability. The first thing a person who is new to disability should do is to accept what's happening and find ways to cope with the situations the disability creates. Second, he or she should discover ways to cope with situations that society is going to lay on you for having that disability. And third—most important—don't blame yourself for any part of it. That's basically it. You can sit around and feel pity for yourself for the rest of your life. And if that's what your bag is, do it. But if it's not, then start moving, and don't stop moving. If you're in a wheelchair, figure out a way to get where you need to go. Demand your rights. We're about to pass the Americans with Disabilities Act, which is going to mean public accommodations for the first time. Don't let anybody dump their stereotypes on you. There are still the stereotypes who tell a disabled person, "That's a very good piece of work," no matter how rotten it was. Because you're not supposed to discourage a poor handicapped person. If a piece of garbage comes in, it's a piece of garbage.

You can't be a "disabled artist." You either have the talent or you don't. A disability doesn't give you any more artistic ability than anything else. Often it is art that allows you to cope. It allows you another form of communication. In many instances, it can be a way of getting rid of anger and aggression, that pent-up feeling. It also can be a way to avoid cloistering yourself away in a dark hermitage to die, to wait for the grim reaper to come and take you.

There is also the attitude, "Look, you're disabled. That's one strike against you already. Why be an artist? That'll be two. It's going to be tough enough without being an artist!" After all, it's only been in the last few years that the art schools have become accessible. If it's a private art school with no public money in it, it's quite likely they won't be accessible at all. So many doors are closed—you're in a wheelchair, you're visually impaired, you're hearing impaired.

So the world's changing. The programs and activities that were once designed in a very patronizing and condescending fashion are ending, and being replaced by highly qualified disabled people, based on skills and ability—not just the fact that they're blind or in a wheelchair or deaf. It's going to get better and better. I'm glad to be where I am.

■

JOSEPH DAWLEY AND GLORIA DAWLEY

*I went to New Jersey to interview Joseph Daw-
ley and his wife. He took me to a café in which
paintings he had created prior to his illness
were being exhibited and sold by the proprie-
tor. I found this interesting, because they were
all in a realistic style, and Mr. Dawley's most
recent work is impressionistic. He seems very
pleased with his new style, and appears to enjoy
creating these new paintings even more than he
did his earlier ones. An extremely successful
artist, he is represented by a prestigious gallery
in Washington, D.C.*

Joseph Dawley:

I've been painting all my life. I just took it for granted I was
going to be an artist. When my father heard about this, he almost
croaked. He said, "You're not going to be an artist. You can't
make a living doing that." He said, "Please, do me a favor. Before
you decide to be an artist, just major in something else for two
years. Then, if you still want to do art, go ahead—you have my
blessing." He thought that in two years I'd forget about it and find
something else.

My father was quite successful as an engineer. Engineers are very technical people—they deal in hard facts. They see the world in that frame of reference. So for him to appreciate that somebody could actually make a living by art was very difficult. I was his only child. He was concerned that art would not lead to a fruitful and successful career. He had no way of equating that you could do as well in art as in engineering, or architecture, or being a lawyer, a doctor. It wasn't a displeasure, it was a concern. Once he realized that his concern was not valid, he was thrilled.

Gloria Dawley:

My father was an engineer, and felt the same way. He thought I was making a terrible mistake, marrying an artist! So the two dads really had quite a lot in common on this. Joe's Dad sat me down and said, "I hope you realize that, by marrying my son, you're going to live a life of poverty, and you're never going to do anything except starve in a garret." I looked him straight in the eye and I said, "Not on your life! We're going to run this as a business, and it's going to be successful, and I don't care what I have to do to make it successful." He looked at me and he said, "Well, you know, I think you will."

Joseph Dawley:

To humor my father, I went to the University of Tennessee, very highly regarded academically, and I took pre-engineering courses. After two years I came back and told my father, "Okay, I'm ready to be an artist!" That was it. It was just in me. I was always drawing in the margins of my notebooks. People really shouldn't go into art unless they just have to—are really driven. It's too heartbreaking to fail if you're not driven, and if you *are* driven, it doesn't make any difference. I've made a comfortable living at it. But for every guy like me, I'd say there are a hundred that haven't really been driven, who could've done something else, who went into art and didn't find themselves. I don't like to see anyone not live a pretty good life. I don't want to see anybody suffer, and I know how the art field can be. It can be very, very rough.

At any rate, I became a full-time professional cartoonist, a good cartoonist, and a pretty good joke writer, too. I had a comic strip called *Chief*, nationally syndicated with about a hundred newspapers. The Chief was a huckster . . . selling "authentic" Egyptian vases with paint kind of dripping down the sides . . .

I was painting at the same time. I finally decided to give up the comic strip. It was really a tough move. But in 1969 I had my first one-man show in New Jersey, in the Heritage Gallery, which was very successful—I sold forty-one paintings. So I started concentrating on my art. Prior to the onset of the Parkinson's, I made a very good living from it . . . several hundred thousand a year, actually. I went along very happily with that until about 1974. That year, the Catholic Church commissioned me to paint a portrait of Mother Seton. At the time, I was preparing for an art show in Texas. But I was shaking a lot. My wife said, "I'd like you to see a neurologist." I said, "Aw, it's just nerves. I've got this art show in Texas and then Mother Seton in New York." Mother Seton had died, so I was doing her painting from the descriptions they gave me. They argued about what she really looked like, that kind of stuff, and I said to my wife, "It's just getting to me, it's just nerves." She said, "Well, I'd still like you to see a neurologist." So in Texas I did. On the spot, they diagnosed me as having Parkinson's disease.

I didn't feel sick. I came back to New York and went to my doctor, Melvin Yard, who was the top specialist at Mount Sinai Hospital. I had a lot of doctor friends. Doctors collect art like crazy. Melvin Yard told me, "You've got Parkinson's disease, an atypical case, there's no question about it."

When I'd heard this news, my first feeling was—well, that's it! I'm going to die. Melvin Yard told me, "No, no, you're not going to die. You'll live a somewhat normal life span, or close to it."

Gloria Dawley:

He could either lose his career or have the brain surgery. That was the choice. Before the surgery, he was angry because of what was coming down upon him. Physically. The fact that he felt he was going to lose his productivity, his ability to be the head of the family, all sorts of things. He was very, very angry. He was unwilling to admit that this was a really serious problem. He had to be cornered and pinned down before he would agree that, yes, he had lost it, and he had to do something, *which was the brain surgery.*

Joseph Dawley:

Before I had the operation, I had gotten to where I could only paint about an hour and a half a day because my shaking was so bad. So I opted for the operation. I said, "If I don't paint, well, life's over anyway." I'll tell you honestly, the thing about the operation that scared me was not that I was going to die. I mean, that's a possibility, but none of us is going to live forever. I was just scared to death that I was going to end up a vegetable. There was definitely that chance. Anytime you have brain surgery there's that chance.

So I had this operation, and went through all this, and when I tried to paint after it was over, I called out, "Gigi, I can't paint!" She said, "What do you mean?" I said, "I don't have the dexterity anymore!" My left hand—that was the hand I painted with—was gone. The tremor was not in my right hand, but I just didn't have the dexterity to paint!

She said, "Well, you've always wanted to try impressionism anyway."

Gloria Dawley:

He was totally incapable of doing anything because of the degree of depression. There was only one way I could possibly see to get him out of this state—to find something he could do and feel worthwhile doing. I struggled and prayed, and came up with "impressionism"—and then had to work very hard to try to encourage him to try it. But he did.

When he woke up from the operation, he felt, Oh, okay, I'm well! So he felt that that meant that he would be able to continue with the same style of painting that he had been able to do before. When he found that he could not do that, he just felt the whole thing had been in vain. It never occurred to him that maybe he could readjust and move in a different direction.

At that point, he had approximately one and a half hours during the entire day during which he was able to do anything at all. The rest of the time he would be in bed. I mean, he was done for! The major loss was that of fine motor control, especially in his left arm.

Dealing with this very depressed person for two years made me just about ready to give up. We had two teenaged daughters. Right at the time of the surgery, one was starting off into college. It was extremely difficult for her. She would call me and say, "Mommy, you know you can send me homemade cookies." I didn't have time. I couldn't make homemade cookies. I was having to tie myself to Joe at night with a string to keep him from going off doing these queer things! I mean, he was totally whacked out! When you have brain surgery, you are definitely in great danger of harming yourself. It is not something that you easily recover from. And certainly he didn't. He did not know who he was, what he was doing. I had to take his car keys away from him, hide them. He didn't know who he was, who I was, who the family was, or anything!

I said, "Look, Joe, you've got to be able to readjust. Everybody can readjust to something." It took a long time because he was so depressed. He kept saying, "I can't. I don't care, I just want to die, just let me die. I just don't want to live any longer." I kept trying to push him to put one stroke here, one stroke there, see if we can't make something out of this, and finally we did. We started on the impressionism.

The big thing came when we made the breakthrough. Finally, after many, many months, he did a painting which wasn't good, but it was acceptable enough so that we could find numerous things to praise—"Oh, gosh, aren't the colors great! Gee, that's great!" Well, then he got really excited. He just went forward, and *from then on, as long as his impetus was going forward, everything got better.*

Joseph Dawley:

It's hard to balance the inconveniences. I'm so much more successful than I ever was. I get a little worse every year. Parkinson's is a progressive disease. It frightens me a little bit. I have to take a cane with me when I go places, because I stumble around. When I get very tired at night, I stumble all over myself. But I don't let myself think about it too much. I can enjoy myself. I can get out and have some fun. I don't know if I deserve it or not, but I do.

What's most important is to keep your life as near normal as possible. Don't concentrate on what's wrong. Because depression sets in, and it can be a major problem.

Don't think about it. I can't write anymore, and I don't try to do it. I'm a better person for it. Also, accept that there are some things you just can't do. So get help.

We have so many friends in the community, I can't begin to count them!

Gloria Dawley:

They were right there all the time. Actually, we withdrew. We changed. They never pulled away. At first, he was embarrassed by the tremors. Getting him to go to a restaurant was like pulling teeth. But our friends said, "Come on—it doesn't bother us!"

It was fortunate my husband had a talent. If a person does not have any artistic ability whatsoever, they could also feel they're a failure, trying to do something that they can't possibly do—and couldn't do before the disability came upon them.

I do think, for such cases, that more important would be to encourage them to try to pursue their previous life before the disability and to adjust, make changes, but do something to go along with their previous lifestyle.

A disability has other compensations. I think Joseph's a much better person, more compassionate, more understanding, less likely to fly off the handle. He's a milder, more moderate person than he was previously. He's learned how to deal with frustrations that he really had not learned to deal with before.

We've been married twenty-eight years. We worked together from the day that we were married. We have always worked on the basis that we have been three things: We've been a married couple, best friends, and business partners.

When we said our vows, we said it "for better or for worse," and we meant it. We didn't think it was going to get this *bad* [laughter], *but anyway* . . .

Joseph Dawley:

She can't say it in front of me, but it's been pretty tough. She took on a tough role.

Being an artist, you can't get out and do the things other people do; you're not tempted; therefore you have the time to be an artist. I always make time for my art—it always comes first and foremost. I love painting so much that when I'm up there in my studio, and it's a beautiful day out, I say, "Boy, I should be out playing golf"—but all of a sudden I say, "No, I should be painting." That's the truth of the matter: I'd rather paint than play golf or do anything. I guess if I didn't have Parkinson's I wouldn't be quite as devoted as I am.

At first it didn't work. I don't have the dexterity in my right hand to even sign my name. It looks like chicken scratches. Frankly, I didn't think that any painting would come out. I had good friends around me; they kept saying, "Oh, they're beautiful." They were probably awful. Finally, after about a year, I painted the painting up there, the painting of Bermuda carriages in front of the ships. I suddenly caught on how I could do it. It began to look good to me. So I got Peter Colasante, who's the owner of the Washington gallery [Calvert Gallery] I work with, on the telephone. I said, "Peter, I've either painted the most beautiful painting I've ever painted, or it's a complete tragedy, one or the other." He said, "I'll come right down and see it." He took a plane and came down. He looked at it and said, "I want you to do me a whole show of impressionism."

So I paint differently, but I think I paint a lot better. It just goes to prove what I've always said: You paint with your head anyway. I think actually, in a way, it was a break for me. Because my traditional art wasn't nearly as popular as my impressionism has been. My impressionism has just jumped by leaps and bounds ever since I started. My pieces sell for $20,000 to $40,000 each. Peter has done a remarkable marketing job for me over the years. He was an antique dealer before, and handled the work of artists who were not living. I was his first *living* artist.

Gloria Dawley:

With the impressionism, his career has escalated to a point where he is being internationally recognized. Previously, with the traditional art, he was just national.

Joseph Dawley:

We go out on subject-matter forays. We'll cross a bridge and both yell, "Oh my gosh, a wonderful painting!" We both see it from different angles. We start taking pictures. Perhaps only one painting is going to come out of this, but there may be thirty pictures taken—each giving different impressions of what we're seeing. The rest comes out of my imagination.

Gloria Dawley:

He has always used photos. But only as a reference. Four or five photos may be involved in one finished painting. He may want to do a fishing scene where two men are sitting on a beach cooking lobsters. But the two men he's seeing were at a bus stop in Elizabeth!

Joseph Dawley:

Perhaps my ability at this style of painting just had to be sent by God. It came to me too easily, too quickly, too perfectly.

That's the way I feel, anyway. I feel like I've been given a gift. That's the gist of it. So the fact that I got sick was kind of a blessing in disguise. I'm a much better artist than I ever would have been otherwise. Besides, I feel impressionism is going to come back as *the* art style. There's just so much to be done in impressionism. There's so much to explore, to offer.

■

MARK DI SUVERO

*Mark di Suvero, born in Shanghai in 1933, is
one of the best-known sculptors in the world.
In 1975, the Whitney Museum organized the
largest exhibition ever held for a sculptor, for
which di Suvero erected fifteen sculptures
around New York City.*

*I first met Mark in Los Angeles in the spring
of 1990. We had coffee together; he was most
gracious with his time, even though he was
deeply involved in the opening of an exhibition
of his work that evening. Several months later,
I interviewed Mark at his studio in New York
City—an old warehouse in Queens, overlook-
ing the East River. I was greeted by a pack of
dogs, seven of them to be exact. His sculptures
are enormous. He showed me the machinery,
including the forklifts, he uses to erect them.*

*Charming, warm, Mark shares much of his
time assisting younger artists. Patients at the
Bird S. Coler Hospital benefit from an arts program he began many years ago as he was recov-
ering from his injuries. He is also responsible
for the establishment of the Socrates Sculpture*

*Park in New York City, which has transformed
a garbage dump into an exciting exhibition
space for sculpture.*

My parents, fleeing the Fascist persecution, came to America
in February 1941. The Fascists took all our money as we were
leaving. We arrived destitute. My father got a job here as a naval
architect. Then, when the war started, even though we were
anti-Fascist, they listed us as enemy aliens; he lost his job and
ended up working in a shipyard, a leaderman because he could
read blueprints, and he was able to help the war effort that way.

My mother was the daughter of an Italian admiral. He was a
member of the cabinet, so she had been raised with all of the
privileges that kind of status brought in Italy. When she married
my father, she was suddenly involved with antifascism, and it
became very difficult to live there. Impossible, as a matter of fact.

Whatever their deprivations, I was brought up in educated
surroundings. My father was a scholar and my mother loved the
arts, so there was a real respect for literature in the house as I was
growing up. When my parents were children, there were books
they were not allowed to read. We were allowed to read everything we wanted. We would sit around after dinner, everyone
with their own book. All through high school, books were my
way of exploring life. I never read about artists. I really didn't like
biography very much. I read an awful lot of fiction, sustained by
this through the California high school system. It had quite an
effect. At the University of California at Santa Barbara, I lived in
a treehouse. I sailed singlehandedly down the California coast.
When you read Conrad and stuff like that, you get sucked in by
this kind of romanticism. When you're out on the sea, alone in a
small boat, you realize how immense and powerful it is, and that
your own means are limited and very weak. I bicycled about 1,000
miles from Santa Barbara to Phoenix and back. So, I had known
the bohemian way of living. I learned a lot. I realized if you could
diminish your cost of living and exist at the minimum, then you
had the luxury of being able to read and live with free time, which

is a necessity for anyone with a free and/or creative spirit. Any young artist finally finds that out. A need for free time to explore—I can't think of anything that is more essential. I call it "transforming." In order to transform the materials that will become one's art, you have to have time not only to work on it, but also the time to dream and reflect. If you're working eight hours a day on a job and commuting two hours a day and having to fix the food and run the house, you don't have that time.

A lot of artists end up not being able to work enough. The real development of any artist is the development of the spirit, and it doesn't matter about a handicap or anything else. In this materialist, capitalistic society you're pointed toward "things," but really, the development is not "things." Two hundred barrels of house paint bought at the paint store is not worth as much as a quarter pound of paint put on a canvas by Vermeer. It's a qualitative thing. And to find this quality is difficult and requires a kind of spiritual, aesthetic development.

I was working as an artist before my accident. I was working to pay the rent, and was crushed in an elevator. I was crushed for forty-five minutes under a one-ton weight, and was told I would probably never be able to walk again. They brought me to Roosevelt Hospital with a broken back and a broken leg. I chose to have the immediate radical operation. Usually, for traumatic back injuries, they just stop and wait . . . but I chose intervention right away. They did a laminectomy on me. They took out all the lamina and then they immobilized me. It's awful, but in the hospital, the thing that you end up realizing if you look around you, if you're not totally immersed in yourself, is that no matter how bad off you are, there's always somebody worse off.

I had a room by myself. Because I was an artist, they allowed me to hang the paintings of my friends in the room—twenty-five to fifty small paintings on the walls, each about a foot by a foot. Whenever the doctors came in, they would only look at the paintings. After three months in the hospital, I went and spent the rest of that year at Rusk—it was then called IPMR—where they gave me rehabilitation. I arrived there in a wheelchair, unable to move my legs at all. By the time I came out of Rusk, they had taught me how to manipulate crutches and full leg braces so that I was able to walk. I entered as a complete paraplegic, and I came out walking, although in braces.

We had a great room at Rusk. The room itself had four of us in it. Lenny Contino, who had been in a diving accident. Then Bonnitz, who had been electrocuted when he touched a wire with the top of his head—he rolled off the roof and when he hit the ground the shock brought him back to life; he was paraplegic. Frank was mistakenly stabbed in the back by someone trying to stab his brother. We had a kind of team spirit in there. Team spirit really worked very well—for all of us. Because, in the hospital, there is so much emphasis on the body, so much about its mechanism—the nurses go around and give you these little cups with the pills in them and you drink your cranberry juice with the pills in order to keep you from bladder infections. One knows that one is really struggling at the limit of life where you can go over the edge and become dead really quickly. In the hospital they're so focused on the body that they don't really have very much time to give to the spirit.

Being in that room was a great help. We used to have black humor jokes . . . Bonnitz came over once. He was able to move his fingers but not with great control; he went over and wiggled his fingers in Lenny's face and said, "You don't know what misery is." That became our joke—black humor in the sense that we were able to laugh at a very miserable situation.

I had therapy every day. What is very interesting about the therapy is that they teach you to build up the parts of you that haven't been damaged. In mat class, you're down on the mats and you build up your arms so that you'll be able to handle the crutches. When they finally got me in braces, and they stood me up, they said, "Now we're going to teach you how to fall," and they kicked the crutches out from under me.

It's important, because, once you fall, you have to learn how to get yourself up again. They weren't doing it for the psychological reason; they were doing it for the physiological reasons, so that you could learn how to deal with the environment. It gives you that whole other psychological part too, because once they kick the crutches out from underneath you, then you've got to make it back up, and that does something for your willpower.

In the hospital, after the first six months, they gave me a space in occupational therapy. First, I did a wood piece and then they allowed me to use torches to do a steel piece. They allowed me to weld in there, but not unless I was protected, since I had no feeling in my legs. They insisted I have an asbestos blanket, made especially for me. I used it over the next couple of years in my wheelchair.

What I did first looked terrible to me. What happened was that I changed from working in wood to working in steel. When you work in steel, the tools, cranes, and welders don't require as much brute physical work. For wood work, you really need a full body, a real physical body, which I no longer had. When you start in a new direction, you always make mistakes.

When I left Rusk, I was able to handle two flights of stairs with my crutches, so I was able to return to my studio although I had no hot water, no toilet on the same floor, and no heat except for one unvented gas radiator. It was rough those first couple of years. There was depression. Depression is something that one just has to fight. It comes with the territory. You have to learn that you've had your life curtailed. What you have to do is pull together all the other forces you have and try to use your spirit in some way to contribute toward the world. It's a difficult realization. This society tells you that you must get more to have a good life, which means having a lot of things. You have to tell yourself that having a lot of things is no longer the most important part.

You just have to take that depression. It's never very easy. You're not prepared, even for the simple things—what one needs to know, for example, to get a glass of water. In the hospital, the nurses' aides can put the water within reach for you. Once you come out, there is a terrible conflict about dependency. The best way to resolve it is to reach the maximum independence that one can.

For many years, I worked alone. I do the drawings and then I draw directly on the steel. I crawl on the steel in order to do the cutting. It involves a certain amount of pain. Then I weld, and I run the crane. I have to crawl in order to get inside the crane. I can't jump up into the crane like a normal human being. But once I'm in the crane (and I've been operating a crane for twenty-three years) I have the capacity to lift weights that are impossible to lift physically. So, I work with these multi-ton sculptures. I pick up beams that weigh three tons. I bend them by knowing how to do the rigging, and things like that. Since my handicap, my pieces have constantly grown so that I have pieces now that weigh twenty to thirty tons, fifty feet tall and more.* You have to keep working at it. The more of yourself you put into it, the more you get out. There's a strange moment of relinquishing when you're working with a piece; the piece takes over, and it assumes its own life. And that's what's wonderful. It's not a dull repetition.

A handicap is traumatic, whether it's a virus or a mechanical trauma like what I had to go through. There is very little training in schools or in society on how to re-form one's self-image. When something like that happens, you have to re-form your self-image. One has to learn to accept the fact that one will never be able to run down the beach. These are very difficult things in terms of one's self-esteem. But there are all those other things that are still open to anyone. You can still listen to a piece of music, appreciate the colors in a painting or actually make a painting. The computer exists for everyone who has a brain that has not been damaged and can handle the keyboard. If a person can change the vision of themselves, then they can survive a traumatic injury without this terrific depression. The depression is because one's self-image has been completely trashed. It's very difficult to reorganize your life. It takes certain practices, which I came to very late. I do yoga in order to handle the pain in my back, in order to direct my spirit so that I can do these large pieces of sculpture. There's no kind of official training for this. But the capacity to learn continues to exist in people, even though they've been badly mutilated. The capacity to give love, to be able to appreciate and to be motivated, spiritual, continues. I keep finding great spirits

---

*I have grown from the romantic idea of working alone to working with a team. For example, Lowell McKeney and I have worked together for over fifteen years.

like Mother Teresa who take people considered "trash" by society and raise them to maximum existence, through this kind of spiritual perception. It's hard to say "spiritual," because the word has been so overused.

All types of things are available to human beings. There's no limit to what one's appreciation of music is if one isn't hearing impaired. There could just as well be a true music class in hospitals, so that you would learn the differences between the baroque and the classical. I love poets. I've dedicated a lot of pieces to poets. I think that they add other dimensions, dimensions that are available to people who are in wheelchairs. You're still as open to poetry as anybody who is full-bodied. One of the things we had in that room at Rusk was that we became very passionate about chess. This was very good for me because it kept my mind awake and I discovered what a furiously competitive game it is. Anybody who is in a wheelchair is just as able to play chess as somebody who isn't.

There are all sorts of therapeutic exercises I think should be part of hospital rehab. There should be a sex education program for people who have had traumatic accidents. People should be trained to learn that it isn't their own gratification that is most important, but the happiness of their partner. One can learn how to cook as a paraplegic—something they rarely show you in a hospital. People who have gone through traumatic injury should be trained to advise and talk to those suffering from similar injuries—professional counseling, but only from the people who've gone through a similar kind of experience. The arts should be used. Art as therapy is able to keep people who otherwise would be *insane* capable of living, keep them alive in a very healthy way. But an art program isn't easy, and it costs money—which is difficult for the hospital manager, who's trying to trim costs.

When you're disabled with a traumatic accident like mine, it's important to become involved with others who have been handicapped. Lenny Contino, my friend from the hospital room at Rusk, has certainly helped me out a lot. He's a quadriplegic, and yet he's able to paint six hours a day despite the fact that he has no success in the art world (one of the extra-hard things for beginning handicapped artists is that it is really hard to get recognition). He got me to come to Bird S. Coler Hospital, where I started this art program for patients. I taught them how to paint with brushes in their mouths and with their feet. There are many who keep at it. One patient, Nayman Taylor, has been there for twenty-five years—shot by a bullet and paralyzed from the neck down. He paints strange religious subjects . . . a prophet walking down the roadway with everyone flat out on the grass, killed—the lion and the lamb.

Patients should always be allowed to paint what they want. There was one young lady who was spastic and on a stretcher. She painted with immense joy. But then one of the subsequent teachers refused to allow her to paint freely. He wanted her to paint a bowl of flowers, which was something that was beyond her capacity, so she didn't want to continue. Another woman could paint with her foot, but she was so ashamed she was painting with her foot that she didn't want to continue, either. It's very hard to overcome what you "think" is normal. What happens after injury, and certainly happened to me, is that all one wants is to be normal. That is the ideal, but it shouldn't be. One should remember that the true human ideal involves the necessity to excel, the necessity to do the best that one can. Anyone who creates art for any length of time ends up with this wish to bring more to the world!

Hospitals are very barren places, unfortunately. Television, which seems like such an easy solution, so quick to pacify people, is really very bad. I've seen people in a hospital—people who've lain in bed for five years—who have only the television. At certain times, you can't object to it. But art can act in a different way. It's a kind of springboard for the spirit. It doesn't matter what kind of injury or what malfunction one has, one can still go through that wild rapture that Beethoven put into his Ninth Symphony. That still exists no matter what level of incapacity one has.

Hospitals have begun to change, though, I think. They put up more art on the walls. They're trying to do something for the emotional part of patients' lives. Before, the psychiatrists were only for people who were trying to commit suicide by throwing themselves out of a wheelchair. Suicide seems to be a real alternative when one is really destroyed. It takes a different kind of support, uplift, to handle it. Support from the family is important. Especially in the heavy-injury cases, the family becomes so important because it's the emotional, nonmaterial, unweighable part of life that gives us all our values. What people don't realize is that the person who suffers is only one part of it; the family suffers, too. Pain is different from grief. Pain is what the injured person suffers; grief is what the loved ones suffer. Just as, at present, there is no cure for paralysis, so there is no cure for the loved ones' grief.

When I got out of Rusk, my brother Hank came down from Harvard for about a year. He would help me by coming over and hauling lumber and steel up the shaftway, moving things around. He'd take off his suit and put on dirty clothes. But there's this thing that I think everyone wants who's gone through a type of traumatic injury: they really desire independent activity—whether physical or mental. People who become completely dependent resent it, dislike it. Those who want it and like it . . . they tend to have very short lives. They quickly become vegetables. The will to be independent is part of one's will to life. It has to do with a flexibility of vision. Without that, it's very hard to overcome a traumatic injury. Everyone who becomes a paraplegic should be forbidden to watch television and taught how to use a computer. There's a terrific danger in television—one is totally nonparticipating, taking it in spongelike. With a computer, you have to work. Although the screens may look an awful lot alike, with a computer you have to participate.

Being handicapped teaches you to use all your unused resources. Overcoming the shame of using things in a nonnormal way is essential to successfully adapting to being handicapped. As a disabled person, one has to overcome the shame of toilet-training. Pissing and shitting are natural functions, and if one is no longer able to control them, one shouldn't be ashamed. Once you're over this kind of toilet-training shame, then you're able to function in the world and give back to the world your experiences on a aesthetic basis. After all, one should realize that everybody who drives in Los Angeles in their millions of cars are in fact in motorized wheelchairs. They don't look at them that way, but that's what they are. It's all in how you look at it. You could drive around on *square* rubber wheels in this city. It would be a little different, but you'd still get there with your modified wheels. *Bump, bump, bump, bump.* You'd still make it there.

■

ELAINE GRECO, DONALD GRECO, AND KAREN GRECO

I had the opportunity to meet Elaine Greco when her daughter Karen's play, Ritty and Jesus Came to Dinner and Enjoyed a Plate of Borscht, *was selected as the winning play of the Very Special Arts Young Playwrights Project and performed at the John F. Kennedy Center for the Performing Arts.*

Through this play, Karen was attempting to deal with her mother's illness and resulting erratic behavior and at the same time show her own need and love for her mother. It seemed that they both understood each other better after the performance.

Elaine Greco:

I remember the first time I stood in front of an easel with a paintbrush. I was five years old. I drew a face. I remember it so distinctly because painting was something I had always wanted to do, even at that young age. But we were very poor. For twenty-five years my father worked on motors—electrical motors, generators, and things like that—for Westinghouse. My mom stayed home until I was ten years old; then she worked in a jewelry factory. So when my dad asked me one of those "What do you want to be when you grow up?" questions, I said, "Dad, I'm going to be an artist." He said, "No, you're not." He didn't want me to be poor. People always think you can't make money as an artist. People still worry about that. I have always felt that artists seem to be happier than other people because they are doing exactly what they want to do. But my father said no to my being an artist, and after he said that I didn't pick up another brush for years.

When I was thirteen I discovered I could write. I won a little essay contest in school. I told my father, "Dad, I'm going to be a writer." He said, "Oh, no, you're *not*." He wanted me to be a kindergarten teacher. I did teach eventually. I hated it! I was the world's worst teacher.

Up until college I had been fine. Then one day I caught pneumonia, and I went home. I wasn't quite right. Something at college bothered me. . . . I was afraid the professors were Communists. As it turned out, I did go back and become a Socialist myself! But at the time that was what bothered me—that the professors were Communists!

Then I had the breakdown—a nervous breakdown. It was diagnosed as paranoid schizophrenia. Nothing suggested this was going to happen. Absolutely nothing. I was a normal kid, I went to proms, I went out on dates.

I wasn't hospitalized because we didn't have the money for that. So my mother took care of me. Every day I had shock treatments in the basement of the Lady of Fatima Hospital. I had no idea what was happening, but they were frightening. "Just lie down." That was it. I was left with tremendous headaches.

After the breakdown, I got on my feet, went to college, graduated, got a job as the world's worst teacher, as I was saying. I got married. My husband knew I had this problem. He understood. He's a marvelous person, who's gone through many of my breakdowns with me, always there, and an expert on this now. Twenty-one years. But he understood the problem. He knew that I was goofy; that was my personality and the way I was going to be, and that was all right with him.

Donald Greco:

It'll be twenty-one years. We met while we were both in college. I was aware that she had had a breakdown. I didn't know exactly what type of illness it was. I wasn't expecting a recurrence. I just thought it was one of those things where she would be all right, because she seemed perfectly fine for a number of years.

We have two children. Diane was born in 1971, Karen in 1972. About six months after Karen was born, Elaine got very sick. All of a sudden. Whatever triggers these things happened, and she was very ill. It took a year to get back on her feet, to where she could care for the children again. I had to move to my mother's house while she was in the hospital. So there was a lot of support. I couldn't have made it without it.

Elaine Greco:

Diane was my first child. When I had Diane, the pediatrician told me, "You need a rubella [German measles] shot. Don't get pregnant again; have a rubella shot." So I had a rubella shot, and it turned out I was pregnant with Karen at the time. We didn't know. It was nine months of wondering what was going to happen. I decided against an abortion. I figured she had a life, too. She had a right to a life. But what really bothered me was that one day she would turn around and say to me: "Oh, Mom, why was I ever born?" That would have floored me. Karen turned out to be the miracle child. She was born with an extra tooth! Which fell out—and I saved it. And that's all. But after that, I had a nervous breakdown. That's when, after all those years, I began to draw and paint.

Donald Greco:

You just have to let her go, because you can't stop her. It's a very difficult thing, because she's not herself. It's kind of scary. I just cope. Just kind of ignore it, try to placate her, try to get her to the doctors, get medication adjusted, whatever it might require to settle her down. You don't have friends over. Since you don't know when it's going to happen, you tend not to socialize very much. It's a little bit on the lonely side, actually. But, you know, I don't really mind. As long as she's good, I'm happy.

My older daughter, Diane, coped with it by shutting it out. She'd go to her room and start studying. Karen tried more to deal with it—confront it right on. Karen wouldn't accept that Elaine was ill—thinking she was normal—believing what she said, however outrageous. It's only been in the last two years, I would say, that Karen has realized that her mother is sick, knowing she has to deal with a sick person. When Elaine gets sick, we circle the wagons. We need each other for support until she gets out of it.

Karen Greco:

I was aware of Mom's problems at an age when I could understand it—six or seven. For the most part the medication she was taking worked really well. Once in a while she'd do something strange. And I'd feel, Why does Mom do that all the time? And why does Mom take all those pills? Why is all that medicine in the cabinet? What's the deal?

The only time it disturbed me was when it wasn't kept under control by the medication. I would watch something happen to her—becoming someone that wasn't her. She hid it really well. We'd start calling the hospital. "There's something wrong," I'd tell them. "You're cutting back on the medication, and you shouldn't be doing it." I would go to see her doctor. I said, "You should put my mother back on the medication." The doctor said, "No, she's perfectly normal." I said, "What are you talking about? There's something wrong. I live with her every day. There's something wrong."

Elaine Greco:

It was 1963. The cold war. I was taught to hate and fear. You hallucinate and you have delusions. Two chairs talk to each other. Or I had pictures on the wall that would talk to each other or to me. Or God talks to me. Goofy things. My father would say, "Your mind plays funny tricks."

The last time I had a breakdown, I left my husband. I went back to my house to say good-bye to my friends. They were upset that I was leaving. I had a piece of Tiffany silver. I held it and said good-bye to it—and this voice, it was Louis Comfort Tiffany himself, came out of the silver, saying, "I'm so sorry to relinquish my claim to your life." I thought, "Oh, very nice," and I put it down.

There are predisposing factors that cause this sort of thing. I was having trouble with my medication. My marriage was going very badly at the time. Then the "empty-nest" syndrome I was going through—my daughter, Diane, going to Brown, and Karen beginning to think about college. A lot of anxiety. And all of a sudden I was in the throes of this illness again. "Reegee" and Jesus Christ came and spoke to me. "Reegee" was Rembrandt van Rijn—I used to call him "Reegee" because he was my muse for a while. I did a lot of paintings in the style of Rembrandt.

Karen Greco:

I was really angry. At that point, I knew in my head that it wasn't her fault, but in my heart, when she was doing all these weird things, like yelling at me for no reason, being really strange, I would get angry. That would be the most normal approach to someone who treated you like that. You couldn't understand what you had done wrong.

She'd talk to my father about his glasses. If he'd complain that he couldn't see right, instead of just saying, "Well, don't complain—just go to the doctor and get it over with," she would go off on a tirade for an hour, a whole tangent about going to the doctor, and why didn't he do it. "I remember twenty years ago when you did this to me, and . . ." She'd really go off. He'd just sit and listen. There was no sense in reacting, because you really couldn't. You just had to say, "Okay, you're right."

I don't know if it's worse for us or for her. I was talking to her

*about it yesterday. I said, "What does it feel like?" She said,
"Well, you really don't notice it because it feels like you're in a
cartoon."*

Elaine Greco:

The time between my last two breakdowns was about fifteen
years. I don't have them continually. I'm one of the lucky ones.
I have it under control. Yes. But, like I say, I have goofy episodes.
Like suddenly I mailed ten birthday cards to a friend.

My last breakdown was like *Fantasia*. Why? When I decided to
get a divorce, voices from the Renaissance came forward and
spoke to me. In the throes of this disease, everything is rational-
ized . . .

During the last breakdown Jesus was with me—the whole
time! He's just there. I can't explain it. He comes to me. I went
to the St. Francis chapel—oh, if you ever need a healing or a
miracle, go to the St. Francis chapel in Providence, and you'll get
your miracle there! That's a miracle *factory*. I pray to get well.
And it works. And I pray for my children. I pray for my family.
And I pray for world peace.

For a while I had an occupational therapist. I made a desk, a
magazine rack, and two necklaces. I did some watercolors.

But I try to put the disease in the background, put it on the back
burner, and keep going—one foot in front of the other. That's my
theory. My philosophy is: Just keep going. You just keep *doing*
it! Don't give up! Just keep going, because it's just a disease—just
a handicap. That's all it is. It's nothing fatal, it's nothing awful.
No fear of harm to anybody.

I only write when I have something to say. I have a muse—
that's a side effect of the disease. I've been left with a muse.
Somebody that comes to me and helps me paint. Selects the colors
and tells me where to go and what to paint. I had Rembrandt for
a while. And now I've got Vincent—Vincent van Gogh. He comes
to me, and I paint in his style. He selects the colors . . . tells me
to emphasize the strong primary colors. He gets tired very
quickly. I paint for about forty minutes and then I get tired. I

didn't ask for him. He's my muse . . . came on his own. I don't know what I'd do if I minded him. Just live with it, I guess.

I don't wish this had never happened to me. Absolutely not! I'm so happy to be a paranoid schizophrenic. It's left me very understanding—I'm very happy to be that way.

Karen Greco:

My mother seemed to not like my friends for some reason. So sometimes, when they would come over, she'd be a little mean to them.

I kind of started to turn against my father. I thought that he was against me in whatever I did. My mom went to the hospital when my sister moved out and went to college. So it was just me and my father. So we kind of had no choice but to get along. We talked about a lot of things, and we really got along better. I understood more about him and what he had to go through with my mother. He could divorce her, but he doesn't want to. He loves her. What he wants to divorce is her illness.

Elaine Greco:

The painting has been very important to me. I've thrown away hundreds of canvases—thrown away more than I've kept. I wasn't sure for a long time what I was doing . . . not sure even how to mix paint. It's like trying to build a house and not know how to hold the hammer. Everything came out dark and awful. I'd do a canvas a week, and when it was finished I'd set it next to the television. *The Waltons* would be on, and my husband would look at the painting and say, "Well, that's interesting." The house got overdecorated with my work. But now I am beginning to sell them—I've recently sold eleven paintings in my cat series. I think of what I do as "soul" paintings. They reflect what I'm trying to feel emotionally—the lighthearted side, the happy side. If I weren't a painter—getting that sort of relief and comfort—I would be a cook. Not in a Burger King, mind you! Italian food, of course. But that's important . . . my feeling is that everyone has a gift, whether it's cooking, painting, knitting sweaters, or making a car run. The hard part of life is finding that gift. And it's essential, because it can save a life.

Karen Greco:

To help me sort out my feelings about my mother, I wrote a play. I showed it to her. I was nervous and worried about what her reaction might be about what I had written: I thought she might be hurt and confused by what the play says about my feelings toward her and her illness. She was very understanding. In fact, I think it brought us closer together, and was an important step in our relationship. When the play won the competition and we sat together in the Lab Theater at the Kennedy Center we were apprehensive, wondering what the audiences would think. We were very pleased and delighted at their reaction. Perhaps we had helped some of them understand as well.

■

RITTY AND JESUS CAME TO DINNER AND ENJOYED A PLATE OF BORSCHT

A one-act play by

Karen Greco

CHARACTERS

ELLEN, *the forty-year-old mother of* EMMA. *She has the mental illness paranoid schizophrenia.*

EMMA, *the seventeen-year-old daughter of* ELLEN.

SETTING:

Empty stage with a straight-back chair in center. Spotlight. ELLEN *stands stage left and* EMMA *stands stage right. Both are an equal distance from the chair, facing the audience. Spotlights remain on both after each blackout. One freezes as the other speaks.*

ELLEN: I'm only from Olneyville. When I was a kid, I had to walk through snow with cardboard in my shoes to cover the holes. Now I have all the money that my husband makes. I can buy whatever I want. I can finally do my real work. I am an artist. I am Picasso, Rembrandt, and Cassatt all blended into one. I am also a writer. I'm working on the Great American Novel. Then I'll divorce my husband and move. I love Paris in the springtime.

EMMA: They had no right having a child. I've been through seventeen years of hell with my mother. A five-year-old should not know the meaning of the words paranoid schizophrenic. I had to grow up knowing that my mother was one. She uses up all of my father's money on crap for herself. I've never seen more silk pajamas in my life! She doesn't work, or cook, or even clean up the house. She doesn't pick up after herself. All day long she'll just wear her green sunglasses, lie in bed, and read magazines.

[*Blackout.* ELLEN *sits in chair and* EMMA *stays in place. Spotlights on.*]

ELLEN: Do you want to see my bruises? I have them all over my body. They're big black and purple welts. My husband does that to me. He bruises me all the time. He beats me while I'm sleeping. When I wake up in the morning, I have these bruises all over. Want to see them?

EMMA: My mother tells people that my father beats her. She shows her bruises to everyone. At first, even I believed her. I asked her when he did it to her. She said, "I don't know. I guess he did while I was sleeping." Whenever they fight, she always brings that up. They fight just about every night. Actually, she fights with him. Last night she threw a fit just because she doesn't like his glasses. Well, I don't like her goddamned green glasses, but you don't see me throwing fits!

ELLEN: My husband's having an affair with his secretary. Every time I go to the office, she gives me dirty looks. Then she flirts with Dan. I really don't care, though. She can have Dan and his problem. I'll bet you didn't know that Dan had a problem. He's a cocaine addict. He goes to coke parties all the time. He leaves me all alone every night to go and snort coke. I'm sure of it. Dan and his sleazy secretary . . .

EMMA: My poor father. He's been accused of just about everything. When we were in family therapy, it was, "You don't wash your own clothes, you don't give me enough money, you don't love me, you never loved me." But lately she's been getting into some real serious shit. Not only with the crap about him beating her, but she thinks that he's having an affair with his secretary. Can I just tell you about his secretary? She's about eighty years old, wears dentures, has hardly any hair left, and eats rotten bananas for lunch. Mom should give Dad a little credit. Another anti-Dad kick she's on is that he's a coke addict. My father hardly ever drinks! Why would he use cocaine? I feel sorry for my dad. We were never wicked close and he can be a pain in the ass sometimes, but generally speaking, he's not a bad guy. He tries to make us happy. He really does.

[*Blackout.* EMMA *sits in chair.* ELLEN *stands behind chair and rests her hands on back. Spotlights on.*]

ELLEN: I have a daughter named Emma who is seventeen years old. How I love my little girl.

EMMA: We used to have to go for family therapy. This was after my first suicide attempt. During one meeting, my mother told me that she never wanted me and why didn't I just move out? She told me that I was a wretched little bitch. I was fourteen years old and I was listening to my mother tell me that she hated me.

ELLEN: Do you know what I told my husband Dan today? I looked him straight in the eye and told him to get new glasses or else I would call my lawyer. Of course he agreed with me. He wouldn't want to lose me. But he will eventually because he is such an *idiot*. And you should see the way he treats poor Emma.

EMMA: She always makes Dad out to be the idiot. It's not as if he treats me awesome. He can be a jerk sometimes. But look at what he has to deal with. I guess if I had to put up with her as much as he does, I'd be an idiot too. Maybe I am, am I?

ELLEN: Dan, that's an ugly shirt! Would you please buy some new clothes! You look like a reject from the fifties. Did you know that the guys at the club make fun of you? I hear them talk about you through the locker room walls. They say you're a real *asshole*. [*Long pause.*] I wasted my whole life when I got married. I paid no attention to my art. Damned Emma was always in my way! She was always screwing up my life, just like Dan always screws up my life. Now it's my turn. I'm going to do what I want to do. They're not going to stop me!

[*Blackout.* ELLEN *on stage right and* EMMA *on stage left. Spotlights on.*]

EMMA: When I was little, I always used to think other families were weird because they weren't like mine. I'd watch *The Brady Bunch* and wonder if a family was supposed to be like them. When I finally figured out that *we* were the weirdos, I was afraid to have friends over. On Saturdays, I never got to watch cartoons like everyone else. I always had to help do the housework. My mother used to send me to school without a lunch. When I was ten years old, my best friend's mother used to make a lunch for me. I remember when my mother decided to go on Weight Watchers. I was six. My mother decided that I would go on the diet with her. So I didn't eat all day and was given diet rations at night. I ate with my grandparents twice a week. I think that saved me from being malnourished.

[*Blackout.* ELLEN *sits in chair.* EMMA *stays stage left.*]

ELLEN: Let me tell you about my nervous breakdown. I've had three, so I'll just tell you about my recent one. My family drove me up the wall. I was just under a lot of stress.

Nervous breakdowns are my tension relievers. Some people eat, others exercise. I have nervous breakdowns. But I don't mind. I just go to a hospital for a little vacation. It's my spa treatment.

EMMA: Let me tell you a little bit about my mother's last nervous breakdown. She was really bad. She would stand in front of the bathroom mirror and talk to herself in different voices. The worst one was the high-pitched squeaky one. That one sounded evil. Then came the laughing. It was this long screech that went on constantly for no reason. The only thing she would do all day was shop and drive around. We tried to get help for her. I spoke to her social worker and psychiatrist. But the answer was always the same: "There's nothing wrong with your mother."

ELLEN: Nobody believes me when I tell them I talk to Rembrandt. I really do. We're close, personal friends. He critiques my artwork. He's such a great, great man. Around this house we call him Ritty. Another great, great man is Jesus Christ. I spoke to him today too. I was in this department store, looking at a dress. Christ told me I should buy it. He tells me what I should buy all of the time.

EMMA: Her dress was divinely inspired.

ELLEN: And then they liked me so much at the checkout counter that they marked it down thirty dollars. Would you like some borscht? How about some nice, nice borscht, with some nice sour cream?

[*Blackout.* ELLEN *stage right with her back to the audience.* EMMA *stands behind chair. Spotlights on.*]

EMMA: Actually, I feel sorry for my mother. She doesn't want to be like that. She has no choice. To her, she's the normal one and everybody else is weird. She thinks that everyone else is mentally ill. It's sad to watch my mother and realize how trapped she is. Not too many people understand her either. Most people don't understand mental illness, therefore condemn her. Some people are outright mean to her. Others treat her as if she were two years old.

Mental illness is a disease. If she had heart disease or cancer, more people would be nicer to her. They would understand. Forty years ago, if you were mentally ill, you would be locked in an attic. Or, you would be placed in an asylum or prison along with the dying, infectious people or murderers. My great grandmother was sent away. Attitudes have changed very little. It's too bad that people can't be more aware. I love my mother, but I hate the illness. When people ask me what my mother is like, I just say that she's a bit eccentric.

[*Blackout.* ELLEN *turns to face audience.* EMMA *stays in place. Spotlights on.*]

ELLEN: You see, a true chef can take a spice, any spice, and put it on a food in a new and innovative way. An excellent example would be broccoli. You take an eyedropper full of anise and drop it on cooked broccoli. Would you like some borscht?

[*Blackout.* ELLEN *stands stage left and* EMMA *stands stage right. Spotlights on.*]

EMMA: Nobody sees how much this illness affects me. I hate to see my mother the way she is. It hurts me that I can't help her. Her illness hurts me, too. It tells me how awful I am when I despise her for not being normal. Then I hate myself for hating her because it's not her fault!

ELLEN: Do these dishes! What are you waiting for? Do these dishes!

EMMA: My mother never does housework. We always have dishes piled up. Then she complains about all the work she has to do. That's supposed to be my hint to jump in and say, "Go lie down, Mom. I'll do the dishes." Then she'll drop whatever she's doing and run out of the room before I change my mind. Sometimes she will stay and try to help. She'll stand around, pick up a dish, put it down again, and stand around some more. That's when I lose it and tell her to get the hell out.

ELLEN: Everything is ironed! He doesn't need you to iron! I iron his clothes. And I do it for free!

EMMA: I can't stand it much longer! Nothing seems to be helping her! The doctors keep trying all different kinds of medications but nothing seems to work. It seems as if she is worse than she was the day before. She needs to be hospitalized but the doctors won't do it. Once she's in the hospital, everything will get better. Once she's in, she's on her way to becoming saner. Not normal, but saner.

ELLEN: Emma! We do not talk about bad things at the dinner table! We talk about happy things, like my nervous breakdown.

EMMA: Sometimes it gets so unbearable, I just cry and cry.

ELLEN: Sometimes it gets so unbearable, I just have to laugh and laugh.

EMMA: I just want to give up.

ELLEN: How about some coffee? Want a cup of coffee to go with your borscht?

EMMA: I don't want to deal with it anymore! I want it to go away!

ELLEN: I don't want to deal with you anymore! Why don't you just go away?

EMMA: I can't!

ELLEN: I can't!

[*They both repeat "I can't!" and begin to overlap. They move to the chair, turn back to back and sit on chair in profile.*]

EMMA AND ELLEN [*in unison*]: Sometimes I feel so all alone.

[*The lights fade to black.*]

■

JACK HOFSISS AND MAUREEN LAFFEY

The way I met Jack Hofsiss was very interesting. I hosted a cocktail party at my home, and many of the guests were artists who had worked on my brother Ted's campaign and whom he wanted to thank for their participation. Among them was a young man who mentioned that he was on the way to visit his friend Jack Hofsiss, at the Rusk Institute. He told me about Jack's accident and the injury to his spinal cord, and said that Jack seemed quite depressed about his recovery.

I discovered that Jack was the director of The Elephant Man. *I had invested a small amount in the play several years earlier, because I admired it and thought it was an important work that should be seen by many people. Jack Hofsiss won a Tony, an Obie, and a host of other awards for his direction of that production. He also cast the original production of* A Chorus Line. *I told Jack's friend that I would like to meet the director, and he agreed to arrange for me to do so.*

When Jack and I met, I asked him to join our

*Young Playwrights group, because his talent
and tremendous dedication to the theater made
him ideally suited to the task. Happily, he
agreed to become involved, and he has been of
invaluable assistance ever since.*

Jack Hofsiss:

I remember first being interested in the theater at about the age of ten. I went to see *The Miracle Worker* . . . and fell in love. Originally I decided to get into the theater as an actor. As a child you don't really know there's anybody else involved in a play except the actors. You don't really appreciate that somebody wrote the words, somebody else designed the sets, and that somebody directed the play. I remember thinking the actors did it all on their own. There are plenty of actors around right now who think the same thing!

When I was just out of undergraduate school, Joe Papp of the New York Shakespeare Festival came down to Washington to give a speech. I had just codirected a production of *Twelfth Night*. He stayed on to see the performance, which apparently caught his fancy, because he asked who had directed it. After the performance he said, "If you come to New York, come see me if you need work." Well, I certainly did! I started at the Shakespeare Festival as a casting director and as an assistant director. I stayed there for a couple of years doing all sorts of odd, assistant kind of jobs. Everybody in the New York theater at some point passes through the New York Shakespeare Festival. It's a wonderful introduction to the theater community, to life in the professional New York theater.

So that got me started. From the age of nine on, I had wanted to win a Tony award, to succeed in the theater. That was very important to me. I was twenty-eight when *The Elephant Man* opened. It won an award. With a great sense of hubris, I thought there was no limit to my horizons.

Then on January 20, 1985, on Fire Island, I was taking an early-morning dip—you know, "Oh, I think I'll take a nice, bracing dip, rather than taking a shower." There were stories that it happened in the dead of night at a wild party, with me doing backflips off a garage roof. All untrue. It was one of those pools with a very severe incline from the shallow end to the deep part, very deceptive. Essentially, I dove into a wall.

I was lucky. The dining and kitchen area was right off the pool. People were in the house, so luckily they came out.

I remember very small bits and pieces of what was actually happening. One of the major problems was getting me off Fire Island. First they came over with just a motor boat, which was an absurd idea. They should have helicoptered me off the island and into the hospital on the other side. Eventually, they took me to the ferry on a stretcher. I remember being knocked around, which must have increased the trauma to my spine. I spent a couple of weeks in the ICU, which I don't remember very much of—just little glimmers of people and things. The first night I was there, my family didn't know if I was going to make it through the night. I had a near-death experience—I remember moving through a long tunnel, with the light at the end. I experienced all the classic descriptions that one has of that kind of experience. I don't know if it took that form because that's the way the near-death experience has always been explained to me, or whether it genuinely took that form in my mind.

When I was stable enough to move on to the rehabilitative stage, I went to the Rusk Institute. At first, I was sequestered away by myself, because I was still in need of electronic life support equipment of sorts. I wasn't on a respirator, but I still needed that kind of private attention. In order to get back into the mainstream of life, I moved into a room with a friend of mine who ironically had had the same kind of accident a week later—two doors away from where I hurt myself! I moved in with him, and that helped. At that point, I was in need of stimulation. Being left alone for long periods of time with just the television on would have stopped my cognitive powers from returning.

Then, after three or four months with a roommate, I moved back into a single room, because at that point I needed to be alone to try to make sense out of this accident and how it had changed my life. And how my life in the future would be changed. The assessing I had to do on my own, and it was not helped with other people moving in and out of the room. I had to come to terms with what I could do with my life and what it was going to mean.

Still, in no way was I prepared for returning home. The hardest part is those first two or three months after you get back home. When you're in the hospital, the anonymity of the spaces allows you to keep at a distance the fact that your life has been unalterably changed and played around with. But when you get home, you're surrounded by all the things of daily life before the accident: Then you could walk into the kitchen to get yourself a cup of coffee or a glass of milk. No longer. That's where the serious adjusting takes place.

At first, of course, there was the initial excitement and the feeling of being very strong, but this was followed by an extremely deep depression. A terrible letdown. I was ready to let go. Ready not to fight a couple of times. I was really suicidal. I was just tired of it. Tired of fighting about everything, *everything*— the littlest thing was such an effort . . . those little things that you just whipped through in half an hour and be out the door.

The beginning of coming out of that, actually, was with Very Special Arts. The program put together the two most important aspects of my life—my work in the theater and my physical condition. That first year they wrapped themselves together in such a strong way that it was a very moving experience for me.

Maureen Laffey:

I was a nurse in the hospital where Jack was. After eight months in the hospital, which is the general length of time for such patients, their support groups are all settled. I thought they were leaving the hospital to get on with their lives. I really had no idea what happened once these people went home. I really had no idea . . . of this deep depression, the kind that Jack slipped into.

I was going to go to Paris and be a waitress for a year. That's what my plan was—just to get out of New York, really. Then Jack asked me if I'd consider going home from the hospital with him. I was shocked. It was something I had never really considered. So I said, "Oh, well, you know, I need time to think about this." *I was really caught off guard. Then about a week later he asked me to take him up to a restaurant to meet a few people— among others, the producer of* The Elephant Man, *and about six or seven other people. At the restaurant, it came out: "Oh, this is Maureen—the girl who's going home with you!" Shock! I thought, "Oh my God, I didn't tell him that!" But then I started taking him places after work—to meetings. And I thought, "Well, I'll do it for three months." I told him, "I'll settle you in, and we'll see what happens after three months."*

I had no idea what I was getting myself into. Had I known, I don't think I would have taken on such a challenge, which eventually turned into a commitment. He had to be dependent on me physically, but I always was conscious of giving him control, giving him decisions to make. So at first, when he started talking about wanting to kill himself, I would say, "Well, if you want to discuss this, I am here, and I am open." I knew that that was the right thing to say. But I was really terrified. The thought of suicide was becoming something that preoccupied him. I also knew that he would probably have to enlist someone's help; I was petrified that the question would be put to me.

The days stretched into weeks. He would sleep from seven in the morning until seven at night. Around seven at night, he'd wake up. That way, he missed all the phone calls that came in during working hours—he just missed everything. My life was turned around, because I was up during the day, answering the phones and doing all this medical stuff that I had to do, and then I was up all night with him. I really protected him. During the day, I would say to those who phoned, "Oh, well, he's in therapy now," when he was really sleeping. I didn't even know who this person was at that point, but I really felt that I had to do this for his sake in the future. It was a real personal challenge. I wanted him to get on with living. Then I'd be free. To move on . . .

Jack Hofsiss:

I'm essentially injured from my chest on down. I'm almost a quadriplegic, although I have much more use of my arms. My hands actually bother me more than anything else—it's a nerve-engendered sort of pain. This injury has none of the pleasures of the usual sickness. No one can make you feel better.

I need Maureen. We're sort of symbiotically bound together now! We didn't know each other very well previous to the whole thing. If Maureen is going to be away for a weekend, someone has to come in and help me get into bed—and do all those other sort of ministrations.

We are tightly, tightly bound together, in the best sense, I hope. She lifts me in and out of cabs. She's remarkable. I weigh between 175 and 200 pounds. There is some physical dynamic between my height and the distribution of my weight and her height, because people of her size or even larger have trouble moving me.

Maureen and I just know each other very well. I feel miraculously blessed that I found somebody like that. Luckily, she loves the theater, too. When she helps me around the house, it's really as a friend, but her real job is as my assistant. She reads scripts and we talk about them. She's with me during rehearsal and takes notes and does all the things that any assistant would do.

It was Maureen's strength and her tenacity and her love and her support that got me through. She kept saying, "Just wait until you do your first show. And then see."

Maureen Laffey:

Josephine Abady, who ran the Berkshire Theater Festival, came by and asked Jack to do a show. It was about five or six weeks after he'd left the hospital. Jack was just so depressed and despondent. I remember saying, "She'll only be here for an hour and a half. Just try to pull it together." I remember being so terrified that she was going to see behind the sunglasses!

She asked him to work that summer—and I think that really made the change in him. I think his biggest fear was that he would never work again. So at that point he started preparing himself. It wasn't always evident that it was going to work. We came home, I remember, from a party, and he switched on the TV as we were passing. I said, "Thanks, that was good!" It was the first time he ever did anything on his own. He never cared; I just automatically did it all. Well, when I said that, he burst out, "Good?? What do you mean 'good'? It's turning on the TV, Maureen. It's nothing. My life is . . . I want to kill myself. Will you help me?" I would say, "How would you go about this?" He didn't know. Nothing was ever concrete. So I felt fairly safe. It was like, "Well, I guess I ought to do it this way—and all you would have to do is, I guess, this."

So I said, "Well, after you finish this show, if you still feel this way, we'll talk about it. Until then, I'm not going to have anything to do with it." So he said, "Okay, fine. We'll talk about it then, in three months." At that point I thought that at least I was buying myself time, though I knew that he, at the same time, was thinking, "I'll show this girl in three months that there's no change." Well, there was a change. We never had a conversation like that again.

Jack Hofsiss:

I do remember a general feeling of malaise and a sort of overall depression. It's hard for me to remember the exact day, but I do remember the change that occurred after Josephine's visit.

Ironically, the summer of the accident I had been scheduled to do a Philip Barry play for Josephine Abbadee. I felt I owed her a show, so I said yes, I would do it. The play she asked me to do turned out to be *All the Way Home,* by Tad Mozell. It's about how this family deals with loss—the death of the father. Although the specifics weren't the same, the subject matter of the play dovetailed dramatically with what I was going through at that time. It was really quite remarkable.

It was rejuvenating—not only the subject matter being so rich and so close to what I was experiencing, but also because of the feeling that I could now get back to work. It was a real turning point. We're always searching for something that tells us: "Go ahead. This is the signal to go ahead."

That play has a very special place in my career. Although it only ran for three weeks and didn't have the attention one gets when working on Broadway, it still, to this day, remains one of the most exciting and most pleasing experiences I've ever had in the theater. It gave me confidence. The rest of the industry began to feel confident as well. Of course, I still—to this day—feel a sense of apprehension about whether I can or can't do it. I still have to prove myself.

But after I did my first show, my attitude did change, because I was sure then that I could function in the profession that I loved so much. In fact, actors who have worked with me before and after tell me that my directorial sense has remained essentially the same. Actually, the irony is I think I'm listened to more carefully now because there's sort of a reverential aura. Since I'm not physically able to demonstrate things, it forces me to be more articulate and more concise in my direction, which are attributes I was constantly trying to hone even before my accident. So it sort of sped up that process. So probably I get paid a little bit more attention. Actors don't resist as they might, which I don't mind.

One of the characters in *All the Way Home* is a little boy, no more than five years old. I had been rehearsing with him for two or three weeks. One morning he happened to be in the parking lot when I arrived for rehearsal. For some reason, even though I'd sat in this wheelchair for three weeks and he'd watched me every day inside the theater, he didn't make the connection. Only when he saw Maureen helping me get out of the car to be put together did he understand that I was injured, that I was hurt, that I couldn't do things. Because I was functioning as the director, and he, as a five-year-old, was not complicated by a lot of other problems, he just presumed that directors sat in chairs with wheels on them. A great, pure kind of observation, one that only a child could have.

To get back into social activities took time, of course. I've spoken with people who've been through radiation and cancer treatments and had to come to terms with the resulting loss of their hair—that vanity thing, which we all want to be able to dismiss so easily—but which is *not* easily dismissed.

One major thing about the social world I don't like is very odd!—that little old ladies love to chat with me when I'm on the street. I hear about their arthritis, their angina—whatever form of illness they have. While it's kind of humorous, it disturbs me because I do not want to be perceived, and I don't perceive myself, as being ill. I perceive myself as having had an accident and being injured, but *not ill*. Actually, I have a kind of adaptable condition. One week, I went to see *Platoon*. Two guys sitting in front of us were obviously Vietnam vets. They were knocking back rum and Cokes, waiting for the movie to begin. I arrived with Maureen. They looked and saw that she was helping me get into my seat. There was a lot of "Yo, bro"—you know. I was a Vietnam vet for that afternoon. Two or three days later, I went to see *Safe Sex,* Harvey Fierstein's play about people trying to survive AIDS. When I went into the theater, I had people patting me on my shoulder as I went. So for *that* evening I had AIDS.

The one thing that surprised me through all of this was the real lack of either interest or concern about depression after an accident. There is much more concern about your physical therapy, making sure that your lungs are clear, all the things that might physically have happened to you. "Can you move this? Can you feel that?" But for the emotional things, no psychiatric help was offered by the doctors who had been treating me and certainly knew my case very intimately.

I began to see a therapist. I talked to her very much the way I think one would if one had gone through the death of someone close. Because there is that grieving process you must allow yourself—very essential to anybody whose life is altered as severely as mine was.

I have lost some friends in the theater over the last three years. They had looked, and depended, upon me in certain ways that involved strength. Having to deal with frailty was disturbing to them. The irony is that now I'm a much stronger person than I was back then. I'm much more capable of engendering in them a certain amount of strength because of the knowledge I've gained from this experience.

Among other things, after the accident I began to savor experiences much more. I began to savor the creative experience of working in the theater. Before, I tended—and it's easy to do—

toward the result, rather than the daily process of working in the arts. The process, the doing, the real essence of the creative act suddenly meant much more to me than the success one gets afterward. Success is very nice, but it is not as sweet to me as the actual work itself. I don't mean work, necessarily, in terms of the Protestant work ethic, but the "creative" work—the genuine experience of working in the arts. It is something that I feel very privileged to be involved with. The friend who had the accident very similar to mine, and with whom I shared a room in the hospital, actually began to walk again with the aid of a cane. And I didn't. But his work on Wall Street is not nearly as rejuvenating as working in the arts is; because in the arts you deal with things that are so personal, so much about the spirit, so much about life on a very much more profound level. So even though he walks—I mean, we have spoken about this in a funny way—I almost feel a little luckier, even though I can't walk.

It's odd, but I'm beginning to see a greater unity in my life. I came to terms with the worst experience of my life, which was this accident, and the best experience of my life, which was the pure, really sweet sense of satisfaction that *The Elephant Man* gave me—the sweetness of working on that piece of material and being responsible for a large number of people knowing about that man and what he was like and how much we had to learn from him. I think it all relates. I don't know if I'm fooling myself. I found a way which has given me, thankfully, a certain peacefulness. The good and the bad have interrelated in my mind. I can't crystalize that into a precise moment, but evolving over the year or two after my accident happened, I began to see those things relating to each other: somehow, the unities were met.

■

TONY MELENDEZ

Because Tony Melendez's mother took the drug thalidomide during her pregnancy, her son was born without arms. But Tony is cheerful, full of fun, and optimistic about the world. He is an outstanding musician, and the music he loves is very much a part of his life. He recently married a young woman he met through his work with the church.

I was born in Nicaragua, in a small town called Rivas. My mom took a pill called thalidomide. She didn't know it would have any side effects. That was the cause of my disability: I was born with stubs for arms.

My mom was surely devastated. Hurt, in a lot of pain, probably saying, "What do you do with this baby?"—you know, what anyone would say. She took the pill, that thalidomide, but I don't feel it's her fault. The doctor who gave her this drug was my uncle. He didn't know that the drug would be bad, either. So I don't blame him. I remember going to Nicaragua a few times, where he lived, and he would come over, drunk, and just wrap his arms around me and cry. My Grandma says that he would show up every so often on my birthday, different years, and, again, be drunk and crying. He was a medical doctor. But the information wasn't out that that drug was bad. He had no idea what it would do.

I was one of four kids—the second oldest—and my mother pretty much just raised us all the same way. I went to school, just like everyone else, though I started in a handicapped school at first, when I was three years old. I didn't leave the handicapped schools until high school. In the handicapped schools, everyone had something different wrong with them—people in wheel-chairs, on crutches, not a whole lot of blind people, but some. I think it was better to be in handicapped schools for a while because I needed the attention that teachers in a public school wouldn't know how to give. Or maybe not have time. So I was really thankful for that, especially when I was younger.

I didn't feel upset that I wasn't going to the same school as my brothers and sisters. I'd go out with my friends. They would go out with their friends. I had some neighborhood friends, too. So I didn't feel that left out, ever. My brothers and sisters were always close. Of course, I couldn't play baseball and do every-thing that a "normal" kid would do. But still I would play their games. I'd be, like, the referee. I knew enough about the game to get into it. I felt accepted, and nobody treated me differently. I think my parents—their example of treating people, and how to be treated—just passed it on.

In elementary school, my teachers would put the pencil or pen or crayon, whatever, in between my toes. It was natural. I would reach with my toes, kind of like a baby would reach with his hands. But my feet did everything. People started noticing. They'd throw something on the floor, and I'd grab it.

In elementary school, I did play music, but not guitar. I played a push-button organ. Also I played an autoharp. Anything I could get hold of with my toes, I would try.

My kind of disability was understood as being part of the plan there, but not really emphasized. They showed you how to fall, they showed you how to dress yourself—living skills. And, at the same time, I was being educated. Still, I felt like I was being kind of denied. I wanted to go to the public high school. I told my parents one day. At first they said, "Well, Tony, are you sure you're ready? Do you think you can handle it?" You know, blah, blah, blah—that type of thing. I said, "I think I'm ready." They went to the principals. "Can Tony go into the regular school?" They said yes.

So I switched schools, did the homework with my toes, took notes with my toes.

Of course I felt strange—everyone else, all of a sudden, wasn't handicapped. They all had arms and hands. It was a matter not only of myself getting used to being there, but of them getting used to me. Some teachers were kind of nervous about it. But after maybe a week or two weeks, they saw that I could keep up with everyone else. Every once in a while they would say, "Oh, well, you don't have to write that, Tony. Just record it, or I'll get notes for you." They would help me as much as they could.

I've always described other people's reaction to me like what happens if you are a beautiful lady, and you walk through a room full of gentlemen. They will look. Maybe I'm not beautiful in *that* sense, but people—men and women—look, everywhere I go. Some people can be bothered by my presence. But you just shrug your shoulders and say, "Well, that's *their* thing. That's *their* problem."

It doesn't bother me. They're going to look. Let them look. Little kids sometimes don't believe that the arms aren't there. They'll come up and say, "Where are your arms?" You let them touch you, or you just tell them, "I don't got none!" Whatever. They're very good about it. They don't mean to hurt you. That's one thing you have to remember as a "handicap"—that people are curious. They want to know. Why not?

My positive attitude is something you learn through the years. When I was younger I was really shy, quiet. My confidence developed through the years. I didn't want to be a nobody, and I didn't want to feel "handicapped." That was another drive I had—to keep pushing forward. "You've got to do it, Tony. You've got to do it."

Fortunately, I didn't have a real big need to fit in—to where I was like *crying* just because people didn't accept me. I felt more like the typical teenager today. I wanted to feel like I am part of somebody else's group—the soccer team, or the sophomore class, whatever—just to fit in, to be part of it.

Since I never had hands, ever, and I didn't lose them, I don't feel handicapped. I don't even know what it's like to have hands. I don't feel that trapped. What slows me down is that things aren't in the right place—like the doorknobs should be at the bottom of the door instead of the middle.

There are many physical problems—things like plates, and serving food that's hot; you don't want to fry your toes. You have to have someone do it for you. Sometimes when you pick up the paper plate you need help, because they collapse. Also, with steak, if it's not cut up. But I don't have a problem asking. If you're hungry, you'll ask!

Dressing is still a problem. I can put everything on, take everything off, but I still can't button and unzip and do that stuff. Brother, friends, whoever is around, I'll ask. Every once in a while at a hotel, I'll call down to the front desk. "Hey, can you send one of your guys up?" I tell them the situation, and most of the time they're pretty cool about it.

I can cook, just like anybody else. You just sit on the chair and put your feet on the kettle and stir the soup, or cut, whatever.

I drive. I have foot controls in my truck—a Ram Charger. There's another steering wheel on the floor. The gas and brake are right next to it. It's a custom-made thing. But it's nothing real fancy. It's basically another steering wheel next to the gas and brake. So the left foot steers, and the right foot works the gas and brake. I've got speeding tickets and everything!

My musical career began when I was sixteen. One day I saw someone tune the guitar. I went home, grabbed my brother's guitar with my toes, and tuned it to the notes that he told me. It worked. My father was around then. He played guitar, and any instrument he got ahold of. He had a real good ear for music. He could play "Mary Had a Little Lamb" on anything he touched. He didn't say, "Try this, do this, do that." It was more like, "Hey, that sounds okay."

Once they saw that I was able to play the guitar and keyboards a little bit, they started giving me some basic piano. *Real* basic.

Music has been the avenue that's opened many doors—not just

in the churches, but in everything I do. I have thirty to forty songs that are mine. When I perform, it's a mixture—from Spanish to English, you know, soft, contemporary, to church stuff.

Sometimes I think this all happened to me for a reason. I get more attention because I don't have arms than if I had them. I think if I had hands to play the guitar, it would be a whole lot harder to have a career. With my toes I don't feel like I'm the greatest guitarist under the sun, but it's easier, because visually it's something very different. Still, if you were to hear me from behind the curtain, I don't think you could tell if I was playing with my hands, feet, or nose.

I hardly ever go to the hospital. I don't take any medications. I don't need any special services from the doctors. People think that I need a shot or something like that, but I don't. Medically, I'm pretty healthy.

I'm getting married in August. I met my fiancée at the Catholic Diocese of Dallas. She was the assistant director. So she was my boss when I went in there for a youth rally. She's twenty-three, and I'm twenty-eight. She's getting a college degree in elementary school teaching, with a minor in music. She's a musician. We hope to work together, maybe write music together. She knows the educational, technical part of music, which I do by ear. If you showed me a sheet of music, I'm, like, "*Huh?*" She'll be able to help me learn to read the sheet music, the score. So I think it's really going to work out just great.

The arts are important. It gives you that extra little *oomph*, brings you closer to other people. People come, they admire your pictures; people sit and listen to your songs; people come to see you dance. It brings out the humanness in people, I believe, more than any other single thing. I remember, in Alaska, I went to a Very Special Arts Festival. There was a group of maybe fifteen to twenty-five handicapped children—most of them in wheelchairs, others on crutches, or whatever. They had this big old giant parachute. They were doing a simple dance where the parachute would go up, and it would go down, and they would be holding on to it, with music in the background. The energy was just incredible, the happiness in the children's faces—not just the children, but the adults helping, and also the adults who were handicapped.

Art is great because it opens your mind, or it opens that one hand that feels rigid, weak. It will make you work a little bit harder. Or if you're on crutches, you'll let go of that crutch to hold on to the parachute. Without even thinking, that crutch is gone.

No matter what is taken away from you, whatever part of your body, something else will take over. If it's not your mouth, it'll be your chin and shoulder, your toes—something else will take over. But you've got to work. If you lose a leg, you've got to be able to get around somehow. Crutches, whatever, hop on one leg. Something else will take over. Don't give up. You can do it.

There have been many highlights. I sang for the pope. That was kind of like the beginning of the football game. A lot of neat things started, many doors all of a sudden came open. It was a highlight, the beginning of many.

Very Special Arts has been a highlight for me. Being able to sing with Crystal Gayle was another. I remember also being in a handicapped program and there was this one girl—deaf, mute, and blind—who wanted to hear the music. I shook my head to her friend and said, "How? How?" Her friend said, "Well, can she sit on the edge of the stage and put her hands on the speaker?"

"Sure, definitely."

On the stage, just before I started, she touched my feet and she touched the guitar to see. She sat there, and when I played she moved to the beat of the music. At the end of the program I was walking out the door, and she was there. I don't know if she smelled me, or what it was, but she knew I was walking by. I'll never forget that.

■

MICHAEL NARANJO AND LAURIE NARANJO

I interviewed Michael, a sculptor who is blind, in Santa Fe, New Mexico. I was unable to go to his studio outside the city, so he and his wife, Laurie, came to my small hotel room. Michael has a wonderful bearing, and his complete composure and inner serenity seem to put everyone around him at peace. He has an awesome presence, and is a man with a remarkable history.

Michael Naranjo:

As a boy I was raised in Santa Clara Pueblo, which is about thirty miles north of Santa Fe in New Mexico, on the Rio Grande. Santa Clara is an Indian pueblo of about 400 people. I was raised there until I was nine years old. We hunted and fished in the mountains quite a bit, and during the feast days there were dances. Indians from the pueblos and different reservations throughout the state come to watch the dances. A lot of people there make pottery. My father, a minister with the Southern Baptist church, was then transferred to Taos Pueblo. I graduated from Taos High School, went to college in Texas for a semester, then to college in New Mexico for two and a half years. I took a class in sculpture, basic drawing, and a design class. I was always interested in art, even as a child. My mother used to be a potter, letting us help her mix the white clay with the brown clay they got from the hillsides. You step on it with your feet, so that mixing it becomes kind of a dance, a rhythmic stepping.

In college, I remember seeing a film about Michelangelo—a film of the *David* and the *Pietà*. The camera moved around the sculptures very slowly, close in, and out, and then back in. The impression it left was incredible. From that point on, I knew that's what I wanted to do. I still have three pieces I made when I could see—a bear, a man, and one of a horse running.

I was drafted in 1967. I ended up in Vietnam. We got caught in an ambush. I was in a little mud depression in a rice field. I felt this grenade roll onto my hand. I pulled my hand back and turned around to look. It exploded. It lifted me up. I felt as if I were suspended. I had been on my knees. I just waited to die. I said to God, "Dear God, please don't make it too hard on my parents." I could see this little red dot with lines going around it. Four men put me on a poncho, and with each grabbing a corner they went running through the jungle with me. I could hear the gunships firing into the jungle. I don't think the medevac ever really landed. They just threw me up into the helicopter and we took off.

First there was just shock. I was very thirsty. But my greatest concern was to not stop thinking or talking. I wanted to remain conscious. On the helicopter the medic took out a large piece of shrapnel from my upper lip. I was trying to talk to the pilot, thinking it would help me stay alive.

We landed at a helipad at the 24th Evac Hospital. They give me this shot and told me I would be out in a few minutes. About a day and a half later I remember slowly coming awake. I heard Vietnamese voices and I thought, "Oh, my God, I've been captured!" Then I heard American voices, and I knew I was in a hospital. For another half a day or so I kept going in and out, only awake for a very few minutes. I finally talked to the doctor for a few minutes. I asked him why my face was totally bandaged. He told me one eye had been enucleated. They had saved my right arm, but possibly I would be blind. And I was.

Well, I was relieved that at least I had my mind. Someone across the way who had been shot was sort of mumbling like a child. So I was grateful that I could still think. Of course, I was angry that I couldn't see, and I was bitter. Fortunately, everyone I came across at these hospitals was extremely good to me. So it made it easy for me to accept what had happened.

About three or four weeks later, in a hospital bed in Japan, a Red Cross volunteer came over and asked if there was anything I needed. I was very tired of just lying there. Because of the surgery they had done, I hadn't been allowed out of bed. I asked her for some modeling clay. Water-based clay. I remember waking up in the middle of the night and playing with it. This became kind of an obsession at first. In the middle of the night, I'd push the buttons to sit up in bed so I could work. While I was lying there in bed, I made a little worm, then a goldfish. Next I made a stick figure of *The Thinker*. Then I made a squirrel with a nut in his hand.

When I got to Fitzsimmons General Hospital in Denver, I asked for some oil-based clay. I made this Indian whipping a horse across a plain. His braids are flying behind him—so are the tail and the mane—as he leans forward holding onto the reins of the horse. I was extremely pleased with what came out. Everyone liked it. But best was that I also knew the potential was there. I knew that, with trying, I would only get better. Someone took a picture of the Indian, and it came out across the country in UPI and AP. The amount of feedback I got from those photos was overwhelming—fantastic. It made me feel good. Once I had made that Indian and that horse, I knew that I could manage it even if I was blind. People wrote and told me how good the piece was and asked if they could buy one or buy some things similar to it—if I could make them one in marble.

After the hospital, I went to the blind school. I didn't learn much there. The instructor in this workshop in the basement said: "We make wallets down here. I'll show you how to lace it." They handed you two strips of leather with all these little holes crunched along the edges and a strip of leather, a thong to sew this wallet together. "Then you'll learn to weave a rug," he told me.

"You'll learn how to make a bench and a nut bowl." I was a little taken aback. I laced about three or four inches on this wallet and I said to myself, "This is madness. I don't want to do this. I want to do something else." The instructor came back and asked how it was going. I said, "Here's your wallet."

"You haven't finished it. What's wrong?"

I said, "I'm not going to do it."

"Why?"

I told him that I didn't want to.

He was quite confused. He said, "But you have to. This is what everyone else does when they come to me."

I said that was fine, but I didn't want to do it. He said that if I didn't do it, then no one who came through would do it. I told him that was his problem. He left to go upstairs to talk to the director.

When he came back down, he said that I didn't need to do the wallet. I could move up a step. I could go over to the loom and learn to weave a rug. I told him that I didn't want to do that either. Nor did I want to do the bench and nut bowl. So finally I was asked *what* I wanted to do. I told them all I wanted was a block of wood, and a carving tool. I wanted to make something myself.

He went upstairs again and talked to the director some more. I was told to come back the next day. They must have talked it over because, when I went back downstairs, I had my block of wood and a carving tool. I was very happy. I sat there for the next month and a half carving a fish jumping out of the water. I never finished it. I'm not sure if anyone looked at it, or if they knew what it was. But *I* knew.

Laurie Naranjo:

I'm a New Yorker who moved to New Mexico in 1973. I had a boyfriend from New York who was going to the University of New Mexico. Things just didn't quite work out, but I decided to stay in New Mexico anyway. I moved into this apartment complex where my next-door neighbor was Tessie Naranjo. As we became friends, she began to tell me about her brother Michael. One evening she told me that she hoped we'd always be friends, and more than that she hoped I'd marry her brother. That was an instant turn-off. I didn't even want to know this guy. He was blind. I didn't want to get involved.

About a month later, Michael called me up and asked me out. I tried to get out of it, but he kept persisting. I was totally surprised. The moment he walked in the room I fell in love with him.

That he was visually impaired was one of the first things I thought about, and one of the reason I didn't want to go out with him. I didn't know anyone who was blind. I didn't know how I would deal with it. But as soon as I saw him I never thought any more about it or wondered about his handicap.

We've been married ten years, and we have two girls—a seven-year-old and a nine-year-old. They're very good about Michael's blindness. They've lived with it all their lives and they're very comfortable with it.

Michael Naranjo:

I'd like to see what my wife and kids look like. But I know that they are all beautiful.

I still get lost in our home, only momentarily, because we have clocks all over the place and I'm familiar with furniture. But if I stand up from doing something in the middle of one room, I lose my sense of direction. I don't know if I'm facing the kitchen, the dining room, the back door, or whichever.

So I have to walk slowly and stop and listen to find out where the clocks are, listen to one ticking. Then I know more or less where I am. Or if I touch something familiar, then I know.

I get ideas for my art from things that I've seen in the past: dances that they do throughout the pueblos—buffalo dances, deer dances, war dances, hoop dances, eagle dances. Once I get an idea in my head, I think about it—sometimes for days, sometimes months—it varies with each piece. When I get an idea, I more or less see it in my mind's eye. It's not anywhere near as close or as clear as a photograph might be . . . it's this shadowy form that I can move around in my head.

Of course, it was like this when I could still see, but if there were any questions or problems, I could look at models or photographs. Today I can't see or look at photographs of an eagle flying, or a buffalo—things you just can't touch. Fortunately, I did a great deal of hiking and wandering around through the woods when I was younger. So I have a fair idea of the anatomy of various kinds of animals. Whenever we went hunting, we had to dress the animal. Things like that really give you an idea of the interior structure, which is important—the bones, the muscles moving beneath the skin's surface.

Most of my work deals with the human body. First, what I do is create the torso. It's generally a very rough, crude form of the shoulder and the hip areas because that's where there's so much of the movement.

Since I have this vague picture in my mind of what I want to do, somehow the communication between the mind and the fingertips is really good. The mind tells me pretty much if it's right, wrong, too short, too long, too heavy. Toward the end of creating the piece, I often use live models, so that I can touch the arms, the legs, whatever area, and see if it's working out. The process is long, tedious, and I don't work very quickly; I don't create very many new pieces in any given year.

As far as feedback goes, I found out when I was first blind that if I asked one person what the face I'd done looks like, they'd say "the nose is too small"; the next person would say "the nose is too big." Who am I to believe? Consequently, it's what I feel is right and good, and that's the way it has to be; because if I rely on everyone else's opinion, I'll never get anything done.

Recently I've been doing some stone carving. The whole process is entirely different from wax, which is very forgiving. But with stone, once you chip the material away, it's gone and you can't put it back. You have to have far more definite ideas about what you're going to do. With wax, my fingertips have direct contact and my fingernails are actually my tools along with my fingertips. But in carving stone, I have to chip away some stone

with a hammer, and then stop, feel what I've done, and then reset
the point of the chisel and take away some more. And as I'm
doing this, I have to keep the whole of the piece in my mind so
I know how much I've taken away. It's kind of like a chess game.

I've created about four pieces in stone. One piece a year. One
of these is larger than life-size. The entire process is fun. I wear
a respirator to keep the dust out of my lungs. I wear goggles to
keep the dust out of my eyes—although they are of no real use,
they prevent my eyes getting infected. I have to wear earplugs
because of the noise from the air compressor, the air hammer, and
things like that. So I'm totally cut off from the rest of the world.
All I'm doing is feeling. My mind is telling me what is right and
wrong. The energy level is extremely channeled. I will stand and
work for three or four hours and it seems like one hour. The time
factor is nonexistent.

I am told, and I think it is true, that there is a fine sense of
balance in my pieces, a softness. This is because of the world
around me, I think—how I deal with life and people. There is a
gentleness about everything I do. I can't run from here to there,
or drive. I have to move slowly because I walk into walls or tables.
My movements are slow. So my pieces have this gentleness, this
soft, gentle movement, about them also. I don't like harsh things,
arguing, fighting. I don't like war. I've experienced these and I
don't like them. So I want peace, and my work will be peaceful.

Art is an incredible way of communicating. You don't need
words. You don't need someone to tell you it's right; it's wrong.
You can create, feel; you can succeed. Everyone needs to feel that
they've accomplished something—sometimes by themselves,
sometimes with aids. I think it's extremely important; all sorts of
positive energies come out of it.

Occasionally I do workshops with children. They are always
asking, "Mr. Naranjo, is this right? Is this wrong?" I'm always
telling them, "It's right and it's good if you think it's good. If you
like it, then it's good. Then it's right. And no one can tell you that
it's wrong if that's how you feel about it."

Working with some blind children in Kansas some years ago,
the excitement, the energy in the children was just incredible,

because they rarely ever get to do anything like that with their hands and feel good about what they've done. You don't need an IQ of 160. It's feeling and emotions. We can express them this way.

I have fun. It's not like work at all.

Of course, I am very curious about the sculpture of others, especially the masters! There are many times when I've taken time off to go places and look at sculptures. I've touched, I'd guess, 80 percent of the significant larger pieces. But it's really a shame what you have to go through to get museum officials to let you touch a sculpture. You literally have to shame them into letting you. The red tape is terrible; they try to make you wear gloves. At the Whitney Museum, the gloves didn't even fit. In Italy, though, they are incredible. They built a scaffolding for me, so that I could look at Michelangelo's *David*. I started from the top. The eyes are just so amazing considering the kind of tools that he had to work with. The tear ducts. And the lips—they're really full, like you can open them. The veins in the neck and the hands are extremely powerful. The size of the piece is overwhelming. I looked at it for about three hours. I was totally exhausted from using my fingers as my eyes, looking at it with my fingertips and transmitting what it feels to my mind's eye. After a certain point everything blanks out; I can't feel any more emotions. My mind is exhausted and can't accept what my fingers are feeling; it has absorbed too much, short-circuited, and so I have to rest for a while before I look at something again.

I don't know if I would have been a better sculptor if I could see. My work might be different, or somewhat similar. It would have more details. But I don't know. I don't know.

MRS. MARY PEARCE AND
BRYAN PEARCE

*I learned of Bryan Pearce on a visit to England
years ago when I was in Cornwall with my
husband and daughter. In a gallery window I
saw a painting I immediately fell in love with.
It was a painting of the little village of St. Ives.
I went into the gallery to buy the picture and to
ask about the artist. I was told it had been
painted by an artist with mental retardation
who lived with his mother two or three miles
away. I never met either one on that occasion,
but two years later I returned to Cornwall to
interview Mary Pearce and her son, Bryan, for
this book. They invited me to their home in St.
Ives—small and comfortable, with a large picture window that looked out on the harbor.
Mary was eager to talk about her son. He spoke
rather slowly. He told me he loves automobiles,
trains, and how much he loved to paint. Afterward, we went to see his studio, a few doors
down the street. It was very well appointed,
with paints and easels scattered about, obviously the working place of a successful artist.*

BRYAN: *I like painting the church and still life, and landscapes, harbor scenes, ships, boats . . .*

My son, Bryan, was born with a perfect brain but it was affected. Phenylketonuria (PKU). It's the result of chance hereditary factors. It's very rare. It affects one child in ten thousand. What happens is that foods like milk and eggs, which are usually a nourishing diet for infants, begin to damage the central nervous system. Now babies are tested at birth and put on a special diet—a chemical in powder form that is sprinkled on their food. They go on with this diet up to their late teens, when they can leave it off and they're perfectly all right.

But since we didn't know this, Bryan had all that food which was poison really. He was a lovely baby, but he only started sitting up when he was about nine months old. There was just this general slowness. So we took him to London. The specialist there said it could be a phobia of some sort, because he wasn't talking properly. For example, Bryan used to be very keen on the old-fashioned steamrollers you used to see on the roads. I would say "steamroller," and he would say some silly little thing for the word, you see. But if *I* repeated that silly word back to him, he'd get annoyed because he knew it wasn't right. He would ask the same question over and over again, a hundred times a day. His schoolmates knew something was wrong. He would come home with marks on his legs where they had kicked him. Or they'd collect outside the house and call up at Bryan, "Dafty! Dafty!"—which he couldn't understand. He would smile down at them from his window and wave.

When he was ten, we took him again. The top specialist in the country diagnosed the problem and said the only thing for him was to go to a special school where he might be trained to mend a pair of shoes.

So from the age of ten to sixteen he was away in the special school for retarded children in London—evacuated from one place to another during the war. He never complained. Some years after being home, he used to ask, "Why did the boys beat me up at school?" He was so unhappy, he told us, years after all this. He should never have gone. If he hadn't, I think he would have started painting long before he finally did. But what does one do? You go to a top specialist in the country and they tell you the *only* thing for you to do, and so you do it.

The specialist asked us why we hadn't had more children. I said we'd been afraid to have any more because of Bryan's problems. He told us that in medical history there had never been more than one like this in the family. Then we had Margaretta, and, of course, we were so thrilled to have a little girl. But she had the same trouble. Margaretta did not learn to chew her food until she was five. She had fits, and couldn't speak. She knew all the nursery rhymes by heart, and if anyone got a word out of place reading to her, she'd shout or make some kind of gesture to let us know that she resented the mistake.

She was a beautiful girl and full of the joys of life and totally different from Bryan. She didn't care two hoots for anybody or anything. She didn't care that she couldn't speak; she would just drag and pull us and make noises—"Ab, abba" and that sort of thing. But she didn't care, you see. She had no sense of danger. We would walk a little behind her, sort of directing her through town.

When her legs were strong she ran barefoot in the sand, her long hair flowing behind, or she would play hide-and-seek with Audrey, a shy, dark-haired girl who came to us when she was fourteen to help out with the family. "Audrey" was the only word Margaretta ever spoke. Audrey was chasing her in a game around the rocks down on the shore. She came around a rock and startled her. Margaretta called out "Audrey!" in this bright, surprised voice.

She was really a lovely character. Her head was always held high, where Bryan's was always held down. She used to go through the streets and people turned around to look at her because she was so lovely. Well, she died at the age of nineteen and a half—I knew in my heart she would, one day. I found her dead. She had a fit in the night and had fallen over the bed and suffocated. I knew this would happen eventually.

Bryan was very fond of her, but they were totally different.

Music was the only thing they had in common. Bryan liked good music. Margaretta liked all the jolly things—*My Fair Lady* and *The Mikado*. If he had something nice on, something classical, she'd take it off and find her own record. This always amazed me—how children do that sort of thing. She couldn't read, but she could find her own record.

Bryan was twenty-three when he started painting. He used to draw little boats on his own. One day my mother came and suggested he should go to a real artist to see if anyone could help him. So I asked him. I said, "I am going to ask you a question which you'll have to think about before you answer, because I shan't ask you again." He thought for a while, and he said, "No, thank you. My only desire is to paint the organ at the Albert Hall." So I said to my mother, "Well, that's that." She said, "Go to Woolworth's and buy a little drawing book."

They were little sixpenny drawing books in those days; on the front page was a ball in red and blue and yellow, and a drum in red and blue, and a yellow cornet at the bottom. One of my husband's staff used to play the cornet in the band. They allowed Bryan to go to the rehearsals and sit in the back to drink it all in, you know. So I got a box of watercolors and a pot of water, and put them on the table. I said, "Don't you think you could paint this lovely cornet? It's like Dick's cornet." On the opposite side of the page was the black outline; so he just filled it in, you see. He was very pleased with what he'd done, and so were we. That's how it started.

He'd do little bits and pieces of odd things I used to give him to paint. Then one day an artist came into my husband's shop. Jokingly, my husband said to her, "I think we're going to have an artist in the family, Miss Heath." She said, "Oh, and who's that?" He said, "It's Bryan." She turned to Bryan and said, "Are you interested in painting, Bryan?" Bryan said, "Yes I am . . . a bit." So she had him come to her studio once a week for three months.

At the end of three months, as she was going away on holiday, she came to me and said, "You must take Bryan to Mr. Fuller at the School of Painting." "Oh," I said, "I couldn't face refusal. I can't because to have your child refused is terrible." She said,

"Well, I'll write a note." So with great trepidation I went up the steps of the School of Painting and dear Mr. Fuller, he's a wonderful man, he read it and said, "Certainly I'll take Bryan, Mrs. Pearce."

So Bryan went four times a week. He was twenty-nine. At that time, he was quite unteachable. I don't think Mr. Fuller knew what he'd got, really, so he just left him alone. That was exactly the right decision. Had he imposed his own ideas, it would have all been spoiled. But he just left him alone. Bryan had always known how to mix his own colors. If you've got that intuitively, the colors are so much better always. It's like music: You can learn to read music, but if you've got that gift of playing it by ear, it sounds so much better.

So he was there four times a week. The students used to come to me and say, "I like your son's work." I thought they were just being kind. But, when I found out that some of them were art masters, I realized that there must be something. He had a gift, a true gift.

It has been so remarkable because everything has been *offered* to Bryan. We haven't sought anything. It is simply extraordinary when you realize so many artists have to go around and hawk their work to try to get a show.

Bryan has had twenty-two one-man shows, eight of them in London. The first one was in a little basement gallery. The last one was in Cork Street—Stoppenbach and De Lester. The first painting he sold was while he was at Mr. Fuller's School of Painting. They have an open show there once a year. Mr. Fuller puts the students' work along the walls. Bryan's work looked quite nice for what it was. Mr. Fuller came to me the next day and said, "Someone wants to buy one of Bryan's." I said, *"Buy one??"* He said, "Yes. It's a lady who's just come from Singapore. She's an artist. She wants to buy the one he did of the old couch."

Well, I could never imagine anyone wanting to buy a picture of an old couch! Mr. Fuller said, "I want to know how much?" So I said, "Well, do you think two shillings and sixpence?" "Oh," he said, "I think you could ask five shillings." So that's what Bryan's first one was sold for. I got to know that artist quite well. She lives in Cambridge now. She's got two oils of his as well.

So that's how it all started. It's been so wonderful, because his frustration used to be so dreadful. You see, he's industrious by nature, but he never had the means or the sense to tell me what he wanted. But now it's all gone. From the time he started painting, he's been absolutely at peace. I never thought I could *ever* be thankful for Bryan. He's such a dear to live with. He's fifty-nine. He looks much younger than that, although he's got a balding head. There won't be any more like Bryan. There's really nothing special about him. People find it difficult to realize that he is mentally handicapped. Of course, he is different. Bryan's had lessons for many, many years. Now he can read—but only things which interest him. He's not interested in the news, ordinary things in the paper. But he can read sufficiently to come back and tell me the notices that are on for the church and the concerts, the times, and so forth. He has a crucifix above his bed. He doesn't know much about the Bible, but he has it all, do you know what I mean? He went with us to church when he was a child. Now he goes three times on Sunday. His one desire is to go to the Holy Land.

The success hasn't affected him, but it's meant a lot to us. Before my husband died, he went out for a walk with Bryan one day, and when he came back he said, "Oh, well, things have changed nowadays." I said, "What do you mean?" He said, "Well it used to be 'Hello, Walter, hello, Bryan'; now it's 'Hello, Bryan, hello, Walter.' "

St. Ives has been the perfect place for him. It has always been a painter's mecca—the harbor walls, fishing boats pulled up on the yellow sand, strangely shaped houses with small square windows.

In the summer the artists flock in and sit in front of their easels at every corner. Mr. Fuller would set Bryan up in some corner or alleyway where he could work. He became a rather familiar sight. If the wind blew, someone would always help him secure his drawing paper. I often wondered if he was being ridiculed. I'd ask him: "Did anyone speak to you today, Bryan?" He'd say, "Only that nice lady with the gray hair and the glasses."

He knows people don't want to speak to him, though that's never bothered him. I'll ask him, "Did you see so and so?" "Yes,

I saw so and so." I ask, "Did they stop and have a word with you?" "No. I expect they were too busy shopping." He's such a Christian that he will always make an excuse for other people's behavior. He's never said that they don't want to speak to him. He always makes an excuse for them.

Bryan won't be able to make out alone. He's under the Court of Protection, which means that his money will be cared for. I just hope and pray that someone will come along and look after him. He would be very easy to look after because he's so gentle and pleasant and ever so kind. He gets his own breakfast—boils his egg and cuts his bread—but that's about all. I will keep him with me as long as I live. That's all I can say.

■

AUDREY PENN

Audrey Penn, who conducts workshops for children in the Washington, D.C., area, has been active in Very Special Arts for many years. Because of this, and her wonderful children's books, I came to know of her work with young people. She came to my hotel in Washington to be interviewed. Since she suffers from juvenile rheumatoid arthritis, she had difficulty getting there, but was anxious to come because her work is an important part of her life and she wanted to talk about it. She is fortunate in her family—her mother is her mentor and a great help to her, as are her husband and children. It was an inspiration to hear her talk about their support. Witty, intelligent, and great fun to talk to, she made our afternoon together a pleasure to look back on.

I was born with juvenile rheumatoid arthritis. The old concept that you get arthritis only when you're an adult is not true. You can be born with it, you can develop it as a child. The condition is very polio-like. The muscles, the swelling, the fever and stuff like that. It was a secret when I lived in New York as a little girl. I would go in and they'd say, "We don't know what's wrong." I can remember gritting my teeth and losing a lot of what was being done around me because I was so involved in getting myself through something simple like standing in line for lunch. That's what I remember about school. Moments like that that are just burned in my mind. I remember it so clearly because it was a battle that I had to go through by myself. A lot of that was a very "alone" time, and that's why I'm spending time with the kids now with this disease. So they know—hey, somebody went through it and made it.

I was very lucky in some ways because I've always been a dancer. When you dance your muscles are warm. It's when I stopped and cooled off that I hurt. I became a chronic dancer just so I would always feel warm and better.

About thirteen years ago, I really lost the battle. Whatever it was was killing me. I would do shows in New York, but by the time I got home from the bus and the subway, I was really crippled. I fought it tooth and nail, just not thinking about it. I did a show called *Great White Hope*. But I knew the end was coming for me in theater. I worked with the Olympics for a while as a dance coach. But toward the end of the summer in 1975, I was doing more talking than moving. Something was terribly wrong. We went to a lot of doctors who said that there were *so* many things wrong they couldn't put it in a category. They sent me to Robert B. Brigham in Boston. I was there fifteen minutes and they had me diagnosed. It's not as rare as I would have liked to think. A lot of children have been misdiagnosed as having juvenile diabetes or MS or other things that have turned out to be juvenile rheumatoid arthritis. Or Lyme disease. Lyme disease has all the effects of juvenile arthritis, but can be cured with a shot of penicillin. You get treated for something you don't have. That's what makes the disease so devastating. Until they finally give it a name, you've wasted a year or two, and you're really sick.

Actually, the dancing made it happen faster. But though it made the disease progress faster, it also gave me the kind of strength to fight once I got sick. I have an artificial hip. I have an artificial lot of things. But the muscles are so strong from having been a dancer that I can cope. I can do almost anything I want, where most people with JRA can't because they're so weak all the time.

Every day, every minute, you're in pain. I take a lot of medicine, and painkillers when I need them. I like to do something physical first. Then if that doesn't work, I resort to painkillers. If *that* doesn't work, then I go to the hospital. It can get to the point where everything else has to stop.

My skull aches. When I get headaches, they are unbearable. But the kind of support group I have—my husband, my three kids, my mother—lets me think in terms of *them,* how strong they are. I have one particular girlfriend who means more to me than life. I don't know too many people lucky enough to have that kind of friendship. I adore her. She's on the phone with me when I'm having one of these attacks, and she'll stay on the phone for twelve hours if I need her. She'll fly here.

If you have ever had a bad flu—that's how you wake up daily. That's what the painkillers work on so that you don't have that achy feeling all the time. You can deal with the bad pain when it's in a joint or when it's polyarticular—in many joints at the same time—the medicines can conquer that. But then there's the big stuff, that can only be handled with braces, crutches, surgery when I need it. You know, the big stuff.

I've been in the hospital every year—for a week or so. It's progressive. I know where it's headed. But I don't really think about it too often. I have termites and they're just eating, having a good time. That's how I describe juvenile rheumatoid arthritis—having termites eating away at my bones and joints. It's not something that can be fixed. You can't slow it down. Gold shots retard it a little bit, but they're still in there having a picnic. They're eating away at the shoulders, so I've lost the rotator cuffs. This hip has to be redone because the termites that eat the bone eat the glue. It just stinks. Next time around I'm picking something else.

The only emotion I allow myself is anger. Sometimes I'm very angry, because it's stopping me from doing what I want to do. But

I never, never allow depression. I just don't. I won't. Because if I give in to it once, I think I'll lose. I'm afraid of it.

More and more, as they're getting older, I explain to my kids what is happening. They know. I don't believe in sugar-coating, but I also don't believe in complaining. So I'm more matter-of-fact, I think, than most people. It's getting to the point now where, if I bend over to get something, I'll get stuck there. Yesterday I was in the airport and dealing with double crutches. After a while, I just gave up—I couldn't walk any further. But my children have never looked on me as handicapped.

Of course, they're very aware that things can change quickly. My son, my oldest, is seventeen. For the first time, he's a little scared. He's beginning to understand how sick Mommy is. He had said, "When I go to college, I'm only going to come back for the main holidays." But I find him coming back. He calls me, he comes back.

I'm angry at the disease. Not so much that it happened to me, but that it happens to anyone. Most children, about 75 percent, will outgrow this in adulthood. But 25 percent have what's called systemic JRA, which is the one I have; it's progressive through your life, it just gets worse. Children go through things that nobody else can help them through—psychological things, like all of a sudden you're in a room and it gets very claustrophobic, you *have* to get out . . . emotional things that play games with you. I go to the parent groups, not to speak so much with the kids, but to say to the parents: "This is what's happening, this is what they're going through, don't worry about it—it's normal and it's what happens when you have JRA."

Children with juvenile arthritis, like any other handicap, are sometimes very quiet about it. This winter, this girl was outside with her class at recess when it started to rain. Everybody forgot about her; she stood out there because she couldn't open the door by herself—she's so weak. Twenty minutes later the teacher remembered and brought her in; she got quite ill. So, you need a little advocacy there. Not only with JRA, but with any number of disabilities. I work with a school for the deaf, teaching creative writing. I telephoned one of the students at the school a few weeks

Mary Verdi-Fletcher and
Todd Goodman

The Cleveland Ballet
Dancing Wheels

i

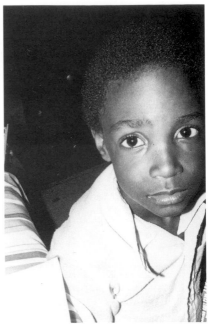
ii

George Covington's
photographs
i The way I see
ii The way I photograph

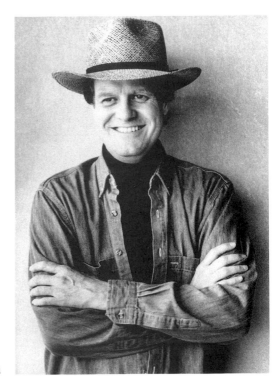

George Covington

Grasshopper by Michael A. Naranjo

Michael A. Naranjo working on a sculpture

Elaine Greco

Cat painting by Elaine Greco

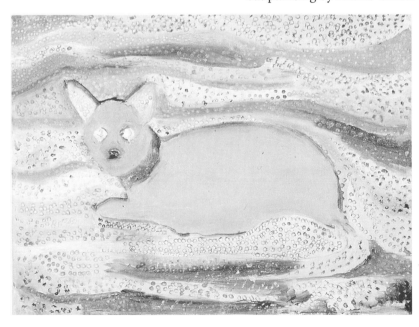

Author Reynolds Price

Weaver Laureen Summers

Laureen Summers's weaving

Painter Chuck Close with *Self-Portrait* (work in progress)

Director Jack Hofsiss with Maureen Laffey

Painter Bryan Pearce with his mother

Bryan Pearce's *St. Ives Harbor*

Musician Tony Melendez with Crystal Gayle

Children's writer Audrey Penn

Mark di Suvero at work on his sculpture

Collagist Pam Boggess

Collage by Pam Boggess

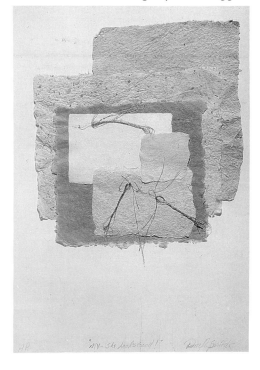

Painter Joseph Dawley

Joseph Dawley's realist *Repairing Clock*

Painter Randy Souders at work

Actor Howie Seago

ago, and no one answered. When she came home for the weekend I said, "I tried to get you at the dorm." She said, "Yes, but we don't have any lights that go on and off so we know when the phone is ringing." I thought, "My God! Who's speaking up for these kids?" That's why I like Very Special Arts—I give them half a day, and then I say "Okay, now you tell me what you need, tell me what you want." Then I can go in and push some buttons. I just have a real good time doing that, resolving problems and troubleshooting.

I'm very picky about the people I select to be around me. I don't need drama—moody people, down people, people with problems. My husband, Joel, is very placid, you know, very happy-go-lucky, but not in a rush. That helps. Our parents knew each other before we were born, our fathers played poker, this type of thing. My father is scared to death. Really, so is my mom. But they learned a long time ago that if they don't want to see me doing things like getting up, getting out, and doing things that really put me back in bed for a while, they don't look. Instead of saying, "Don't do it," they close their eyes and they don't look. And that's what I want. Because everything I do, I get a reaction. Tomorrow will be a very tough day for me because I was sitting here. But I would never in a million years think not to. But if you called and asked if I could come back tomorrow, I'd have to say, "It takes three days to recuperate. Can I come back in three days?" But they don't stop me anymore. They don't put on the brakes. Last year Joel got very frightened and went to my doctor and said, "Do something." The doctor just looked at him and said, "There's no way." When it stops me it stops me. I'm allergic to my adrenaline. That's the basis for the whole disease.

I've given in a little. I wanted to ski this winter and the opposition was so enormous that I dropped it. I stand at the top of the hill. Someone pushes and down you go. The problem is if I fall, I've got all sorts of metal and steel in me that could go in any direction.

But it's important to me to take up challenges. Last September, where my kids go to gymnastics school, they knew I had worked with gymnasts before. I was asked if I could give some advice to kids on the team. Well, it started as giving advice, and then I actually discovered that I could show them a couple of moves if I used my crutches. I built up my strength. It has progressed now to the point that I rarely use crutches at all. I'm really able to walk through whole dances in front of them. But it destroyed more joints in one year than have been destroyed over the last four or five years. Psychologically, it was wonderful. Physically, it was bad. I give you the choice. Wouldn't you rather be psychologically healthy and nix the physical, rather than the opposite?

I make a living out of having a good time. Wherever I go I find something to write about. I work with children's books. I have a book coming out on dinosaurs. I go to the schools and talk at the elementary school level as well as the upper. I go and we just "wing it." Whatever class is brought in to me, I take that age group, and I size them up as to what they want to hear for the day. I try to get them interested in books and in writing. A lot of kids' first comment is, "I don't have anything to write about." Of course they have a million things, from the time they wake up to the time they get to school. They just don't know how to look, how to see it.

I started wanting to write when I was a kid. When I got too sick to work in dance, it always came back to writing.

Without writing, I would have been dead a long time ago. Because, no matter how I feel, if I can go to the computer, I'm okay. And very often, when I'm too tired, I'll go to the computer, and it revives me. There's something about the creative process that gets the positive adrenaline going. That way I don't feel the pain. Writing is painful for me, but it's also my escape. It helps me psychologically.

I'd say three days out of the week I'm in bad shape. But if I know I have a school date, then I rest a lot for two days beforehand. I don't push at the computer, I don't push anything, so that I'll have the strength. Because the day after the school visit—like today—I can't walk. So for me to do a school really takes four days.

I go to the school when they open at 9:00. I sit in the library, in the reading center, in a rocking chair, and I have each grade brought to me. I do six lectures. Normally, I have enough medicine in me so that I can really put on a show. Now it's getting harder. By the time lunch comes, I am really starting to feel it. The teachers can sense it. I tell the children at that point that I'm going to start talking a little lower. I point to my crutches, and I tell them why I use them. I let them ask questions. Only once did I leave a school early. Last week, for the first time in ten years, I came home from school. I was in so much pain I couldn't function.

I try to set an example. Two years ago, I had just finished with a sixth grade. At the very end of the class, as the kids were leaving, the teacher brought over this child, very sickly looking. She introduced me. She said, "Beatrice has juvenile rheumatoid arthritis, just like you." The little girl looked at me and said, "You know, everybody's been telling me I can't get married, I can't have kids, I can't have a career. You're doing it all, so I don't see why I can't." So that makes it worthwhile.

I tell the children if there are people in their lives who are negative, that's the time to be rude. That's the time to say, "Look, I have to be 'up.' I have to have positive energy around me." When I talk to the parents, I tell them to support their children in this.

What is so neat about Very Special Arts is that they don't emphasize what the child can't do; they emphasize what the child can do. Children are not brought there just to watch other handicapped people do things. They are brought there to learn—this is something *you* can do too.

If I had the personality of some people I have met, I wouldn't have made it. I was just very lucky. My mother is just the Rock of Gibralter, and that's how I was raised. She would never feel sorry for herself. My mother has gone through more than any person should have to handle, but she's always done it with tremendous grace and strength. She was my role model.

Still, I'd like to think that if I didn't have JRA I'd still be dancing. There's nothing good I can say about this. Absolutely nothing. The only thing I get out of it now is if through my example the kids can say, "I can do it because somebody else did"—then I'm glad. That is the *only* good thing that has come out of this. I haven't learned anything about life. Not a thing. Perhaps the only thing is that everybody can't adjust. It's too bad . . . that you have people to whom this is going to happen, and they're going to be defeated.

The arts have saved me, the arts make it okay; they give me something to fight with. If you're going to have whatever it takes to make it in the arts, even as a good amateur, then you've got a will that somebody else might not have. You're not going to find a defeatist—not in the arts. Therefore, it follows that you can't be a defeatist about *anything* that's happened to you.

So I'm always very pleased when I wake up. It's kind of a surprise, like, I'm still here. I accept the bad days. I don't go out. I don't greet people. I don't pretend. I just stay home and do what I have to do to get through it. I have never been down—I don't think—a day. Of course, there are times. I lost a month last year when I was doing a book on the pirate Blackbeard. I spent a month holding my jaw from the pain. My notes don't make sense, my tapes don't make sense—because I was in so much pain that I just sat grabbing my jaw. Finally it got to the point that they took an MRI [magnetic resonance imagining] and found out how to stop the pain. But I was in pain for so long it was like a shock *not* to have it. So I really lost time last year. That's the kind of thing that I don't show kids, that I don't take to school; that's the kind of thing that I don't bring up. Yes, there's the dark side of it—and maybe I'm doing them an injustice by not talking about it, because it's confusing to parents who say, "You have JRA, why are you like this? Cheerful. Carrying on. My poor kid's at home crying because he's in so much pain." But that's my way of getting through the day, the month, the year—whatever it's going to take to get to the end of this attack, to finish this really bad period. Why, I had an eighteen-month period where I couldn't use my fingers, I couldn't walk, I couldn't do anything. So I tape-recorded some ideas for plots that I wanted to write about when I was better.

So, that's tough. It gets very involved when I'm going through a bad time. But my friends—honestly—I go through a period like that and these people start showing up with suitcases saying, "I can stay a week."

But I have been able to circumvent the great loss in my life, dancing, and transfer it to another art form. I need the kind of kinetic energy you find in the arts. If you take somebody that has been housebound to a park and then home again, they're going to go back. But if you take them to a concert or something involved with the arts, they're going to *thrive* on it. It will help change their whole outlook, if you can get people into the art environment.

There is so much truth about the power of mind over medicine. Yes, I need the medicine, the pins, the surgery, all these things that have been put in me, but so long as the mind is refreshed all the time, then . . . it sort of feeds the soul.

There's something else, too. I think people with disabilities are forced to look at themselves harder than most people do. Therefore, they can reach down deeper and be creative. Sometimes this occurs to me—that people without handicaps have a handicap.

■

REYNOLDS PRICE

Reynolds Price was born in North Carolina in 1933. In the many years of his literary career he has published short stories, poems, plays, essays, and translations. In 1988, he became a member of the American Academy and Institute of Arts and Letters. At present he teaches at Duke University (where he was an undergraduate) for one semester each year. He has been confined to a wheelchair since 1984, when he underwent the first of three operations for spinal cancer.

I interviewed Reynolds at his lovely home in a wooded area near the university. His house, cozy and warm, books everywhere, is arranged so that he can move about in his wheelchair quite easily. Each year, a young aspiring author lives there with him, helping with the chores, and in return receives the kind of advice that any writer would treasure. It works out happily for both parties.

I discovered that I had this spinal cancer in 1984. I began to develop a slight problem walking. It felt like I was a little drunk.

I would say to myself, "I can't let anyone know I'm not walking quite straight; I must be very careful now, as I walk toward the car while other people are looking." Since I was the world's laziest person in terms of exercise, I thought, "My God, I'm fifty-one years old; I've got to join a gym and get in control of myself." Then very quickly, in a matter of about six weeks, balance and walking straight became quite a problem. I thought, "Oh, my God, I have multiple sclerosis," because I have a couple of friends who had MS for years. So I was admitted to Duke University Medical Center. Initially they rather suspected that might be what it was, but after two or three days of tests, they discovered this colossal tumor in my spinal cord—one of the largest they've ever seen. My problem was interesting. Most brain and spinal cord tumors don't metasticize. So good news, bad news. The bad news: You've got a tumor, there's a fire in the control room. The good news: Though it can grow, it won't spread. One of the very strange things about mine was that it had managed to get to this enormous size in my spine without ever being discovered. The doctor said it was about the size of a pencil. Since a spinal cord is about the size of your thumb, you can imagine how huge that is. Spinal cord tumors are most frequently found in children; they are very often congenital. In fact, when I looked back at my childhood, I remembered having these very mysterious convulsions which they never managed to diagnose. They stopped when I was about four or five years old. I'd a strange coordination and balance problem all along, which suggests the strong possibility that the tumor may have been there all my life. For whatever reason, it took off at some point, and got bigger—ten inches long, from the upper part of my neck down. When they operated, on June 7, 1984, they found there was basically nothing they could do, since the tumor had completely implicated the nerves of the spinal cord. So they sewed me back up.

Then they did five weeks of very intense radiation—about forty-five seconds of radiation a day. I have described it as going to Hiroshima for lunch every day for five weeks. It seems like nothing while it's happening, but the next thing you know, you're just beginning to die. They warned me when they did the radiation that one of the dangers of attempting to burn the tumor was that I might wind up paraplegic. Within a couple of weeks I very rapidly began losing control of my legs. Over the next year, the summers of eighty-four and eighty-five, I wound up being totally paralyzed in my legs. I went into the rehabilitation center of Duke and spent a month there, learning how to deal with this situation. At that point, there's always this big denial phase that one has to go through: You say, "No, no, no—I'm going to walk. This is just a weakness, and I'm going to overcome it." Then the time finally comes when you have to say, "I just don't have these legs any-more. I have to learn how to roll around and rearrange my house and get human help." But that whole year, from June 1984 to June 1985, was certainly the strangest, most complicated, difficult time of my life.

After that, the radiation did indeed arrest the tumor. But then it began returning. The great fear was that it would start up again up in my neck, that I would lose the use of my hands and become a quadriplegic. Fortunately by that time an amazing sort of ultra-sonic laser scalpel had become available which permitted my surgeon to go in to remove the tumor. For the three years since the surgery, all my scans have been completely clear.

Of course, in the early stages I was terrifically depressed. I knew you weren't supposed to ask God questions, even when things got really bad. But I finally said, "How much more of this is there going to be?" I began to think, "My God, am I going to die younger than my father?" He had died when he was fifty-four years old. I was fifty-one. Fortunately I was surrounded by enor-mously supportive family and friends, who were tough, realistic people. They weren't saying, "Ignore this, you're going to be fine." They were saying, "This is going be a hell of a struggle."

One thing that moved and impressed and amazed me were a few people, mostly women, who would come by or phone or write and just say quite clearly, as though they had some sort of special knowledge, that I wasn't going to die. They would say it that way: it wasn't some sort of fancy or sugar-sweet cuteness. It was, "Reynolds, you aren't going to die; you're going to have to learn how to deal with how to use this."

One of my visitors was in the process of dying of uterine cancer herself. She called me up one Sunday and said, "You are not going to die of this. Go and read the Ninety-first Psalm," which has that wonderful thing about "He shall give his angels charge over thee, to keep thee in all thy ways."

By that time, the first four hard months, I couldn't work at all. I had been writing a novel, *Kate Vaiden*. I had written about a third of it. That broke down. I just basically sat around the house, tried to read, and reverted to a childhood love of drawing. Watched lots of movies on the Betamax. Then five months into this weird recuperation, a college in Arkansas, Hendrix College, suddenly called me and asked if they could commission me to write a play for their drama students. I'd given them a couple of readings out there. I said, "Well, you need to know that I may not live to finish." They replied, "If you're willing to take the risk, we are."

So I went out and began working on an idea about the great marital crisis in the life of a young couple who were very much like my parents—about the husband's drinking, and paying far too little attention to his wife in the first year of their marriage. I survived, I finished it, I was feeling better.

I went out to Hendrix and worked with the students in rehearsals. The writing of the play, somehow, cranked me back up as a worker, as a writer. I went back and finished *Kate Vaiden*.

That call from Hendrix was a real sort of angel message. I just thought, "This is not accidental, get to work," and so I did. It happened as easily as that.

Of course, a great deal of physical difficulty was going on; it's an amazing process to go slowly through the loss of your legs. But once I got in the chair, I said to myself, "Okay, Reynolds, you're a paraplegic. You're somewhat paralyzed, as Franklin Roosevelt was. Start living your life and learning how to live it."

Now, I simply never think about standing up and walking again. I used to think that if I could just stand up for thirty seconds, I'd surrender a year of my life. Now it simply never dawns on me.

I have a lot of constant pain, but I take no pain medications.

I take a muscle relaxer. I took methadone for about three years in the hope of getting rid of the pain; all methadone did for me was make me groggy most of the time. It had very little effect on the pain. Finally, when the pain got almost intolerable, my surgeon suggested I see the biofeedback people at the Duke hospital, and that helped a good deal. I turned out to be good at the kinds of concentration required for biofeedback, so they sent me on to a hypnotist in the Department of Psychiatry. Hypnosis became the chief means by which I learned to handle pain, to just say, Okay, so what? So I'm in pain. The pains, which resulted from my spinal cord having been cut into three times and radiated, cooked for five weeks, are not killing me, not signaling that I should race to the emergency room. So I just have to learn to say, "Yeah, I hurt like hell," but to make it seem very peripheral, sort of like something's on fire out in the yard. It's not like having a fire in the living room.

Initially what the hypnotist did was this fifteen-minute routine in which he used very tranquil images of sinking down, relaxing, resting, imagining me in very pleasant places, getting me into that very receptive state of complete relaxation, and then just basically telling me to imagine some part of my body of which I was more conscious than I wished as "a shape." I would always see my spine and my two legs, almost like a twisted tuning fork. Then he would say, "Project that shape toward the horizon until it's only a point of light. In your mind, there's a rotary switch; now turn the switch until the light almost disappears." The first time he did it, I was scared to death, it felt so good.

He made me a tape of his voice doing that; then he sort of weaned me off the tape onto my own. Actually, I don't do the routine very often anymore because I have convinced my conscious mind to just stop worrying. I mean, we're taught from the moment we're born that pain means trouble, get to the doctor, get to Mother, get to the emergency room. My pain cannot be helped, and it doesn't need help.

It's not so much that I'm going to learn to love it, but it's there and I'm willing not to object to it. There are times when I overextend myself or it gets hooked up with the weather and electrical storms; I get much more spastic. It gets annoying at times, but I have learned reasonably well to ignore it.

In the beginning, I just couldn't sleep for anxiety, and depression. I would go to sleep at 8:00 at night and wake up at 3:00 in the morning and then just lie there in the dark and imagine all these awful scenarios. Very quickly, once I got to work, that faded away. I have a tremendous amount of energy. I work about six or eight hours a day; I see friends at night or watch a movie, and then keep working until daybreak.

I'm someone who was born a writer, someone who all my life has been intensely religious in a very sort of odd, exhibitionistic way. When this great express train collided with my life in 1984— well, it's hard to talk about it without sounding like some dreadful TV evangelist, especially in the middle of this awful evangelist plague in the country, but I think that kind of faith was the strongest single support I had.

Of course, I did have these black periods of waking up at 3:00 in the morning and thinking, "Okay, this is it, you're dying." What I didn't know, thank God, was that my surgeon had told my brother that I probably had five to six weeks to live. He was wise enough to know that if he told me I would have folded my hands and counted six on the calendar and obeyed the doctor, like the well-brought-up boy I'd always been. The pathology report on the tumor was that it was an extremely rapid, malignant growth. So it was; it just didn't get me. The weekend before radiation I had this experience. I don't think of it as a dream. I think I was awake. I had been in Israel just a few months before, near the Sea of Galilee and through those villages where Jesus had worked and done the healings. In this vision, I had this very clear image of me with Our Lord in the sea. I had been tattooed on my back for the actual aiming of the X-ray. In the vision, I could see Him pouring this water over my head and my back. I could see my back, and this long eleven-inch incision, with a box drawn around it in gentian purple so the radiologists would know exactly where to aim the zapper. He said to me, "Your sins are forgiven." That's not what I wanted to hear. So He started to walk toward land. I asked, "Am I also healed?" He said, "If you insist." I decided to

take that as a fact that I was indeed healed. I was lying in bed wide
awake and I just simply saw this event happen.

I wrote this poem about it:

Vision

I'm sleeping with Jesus and his twelve disciples
On the vacant east shore of Lake Kinnereth—
The Sea of Galilee—near where he exorcised
The demon Legion. We're flat on the ground,
Cocooned in clothes. Mine are light street clothes
(Apparently modern, theirs are classic robes);
And I wake early, well before dawn—
Hour of the worm that desolates hope.
I give it long minutes to line another tunnel
With eggs that will yield the next white wave
Of ravenous heirs.
⠀⠀⠀⠀⠀⠀⠀⠀⠀Then I roll to my right side
And see in the frail dark that Jesus has somehow
Moved nearer toward me. I listen to hear
If he sleeps or wakes.
⠀⠀⠀⠀⠀⠀⠀⠀⠀Then we stand in the lake,
Both bare to the waist. Light creeps out toward us
From the hills behind; the water's warm.
I see us both as if from a height.
My spine is scored by a twelve-inch incision,
Bracketed now by gentian-purple
Ink that's the map for X-ray therapy
Due in two days. Jesus's beard
Is short and dry, though with both broad hands
He lifts clear water and pours it down
My neck and scar.
⠀⠀⠀⠀⠀⠀⠀⠀⠀Then we climb toward shore.
I get there first and wait on the stones—
We're still the only two awake.
Behind me he says "Your sins are forgiven."
I think "That's good but not why I came."
I turn and say "Am I also cured?"
He comes close but looks down. He says "That too,"
Then wades strong past me and touches land.

Of course, I certainly wouldn't say that I have gone whistling through my days. There were times of tremendous depression, but never any thought of surrendering. I was helped by friends who came to help me. Dan ———, who was on a Rotary Fellowship in South Africa, phoned me from South Africa after my first surgery. "You're going to need me when this is over." I said, "I don't think so." "You are," he said, and he flew back from South Africa and lived in this house for eighteen months. He made me want to live. He was just twenty-two years old, this young man with a fantastic gift of grace to give. I made him leave. I finally said that he must set a date to leave because it was clear that I would always need someone living in this house to get me through the parts of my life that I can't manage on my own. So we set a date. With some difficulty I found another person to move in. And since then, I've had this wonderful succession of these angels, literally these unbelievably selfless, life-giving people . . . five people now, and just when one's term is about to expire, the next wonderful person has turned up. They've almost all been people interested in writing; they've taken a year of their lives to stay in this quiet house in the country and help me get in and out of bed, the shower, the car; they share my life; they do the cooking, and those other things that are dangerous for me to do. It's worked out wonderfully for all.

My life has become two very paradoxical things. It's become very still, in the physical sense, because of being in this chair. But it's also active in a more focused way. I was always someone who stayed at home and alone a great deal of the time—partly the heritage of being an only child until I was eight. I always needed time alone. Writing is very soft work, like most forms of creative art, so I was never some kind of Mexican jumping bean, hopping around the world. I traveled to Europe and the Middle East, wherever I wanted to, but most of the time I was here in this house. Now I'm here even more than ever, basically all day, working here at the processor, tapping away. Initially I didn't want to go out at all. I got very agoraphobic. If you're in this condition, there are all kinds of problems. I mean going to the bathroom, you've got to learn a whole new way of doing that—

just everything, your clothing, your dress, the way you eat a meal; it's like having to learn Chinese at the age of fifty-one. But, damn it, you either learn it, or you die. Or you become someone who is so wretched and miserable and mean that no one can stand to be around you.

I call it my afterlife, this new life I have; it sounds almost unforgivably buoyant to say so. But in a lot of ways, these last five years have been the best part of my life—once I got through that very narrow keyhole of the first year of pain and rapid paralysis.

I think it's because I'm working better. Personal relations seem better. I remember just a couple of years ago, two of Franklin Roosevelt's sons were talking on some morning show about their father. The interviewer asked, "How did your father change after his paralysis?" FDR, Jr., said, "The main thing we perceived as children was that it made him a much more patient person." That's certainly so. You either become enormously patient or you go insane. The powerlessness of it is extremely oppressive initially. If a picture is crooked on the wall, you can't get over there and straighten it. But a kind of peaceful mellowness began, which continues, and which I'm almost afraid to mention for fear that it'll go away if I look it in the eye.

Of course, I could lose my hands if the tumor ever returned. I don't think it's going to. When I spoke with my surgeon, after my annual scan, he said, in the way that doctors insist on doing, that everything was completely clear. I'm convinced that we will have to deal with this tumor eventually. I'd never let him know that I was aware he had once given me five to six weeks. This time I said, "Alan, you thought I was dead five years ago." There was a long pause and he said, "You're right."

The mental state is enormously important.

I don't think this is the end of me. I've never been much of a churchgoer. I tend not to see eye to eye. I've always hated the judgmental part of branches of Christianity. So many of the churchgoers I've known seem to be in the business of being district attorneys more than anything else; they're always prosecuting people. Maybe I don't have enough sense of sin, but it seems to me the main thing that Jesus says about God is that God is in the business of forgiveness. It's interesting: In that "experience"

I had, the first thing Jesus said was, "Your sins are forgiven." But when you nail religion down and say you can't eat chicken on Wednesday or whatever, that's when I start having terrific problems.

It's very hard to know what I would have done, if I hadn't been up to the crown of my head in a kind of work which I absolutely love. My work comes into me, and in the last five years it's been coming in strong and clear and unceasing. I've had to declare vacations and make myself stop. Publishers really can only publish you about once every six months. I've always been a productive writer. I published a book on the average of once every other year. But in the last five years I've published at least five books, finished three more, and that's a fast clip for my age.

At first I was suspicious that this was quantity as opposed to quality. But the books have been well received and my own sense convinces me that this is good stuff, as good if not better than what I've done all my life at a slower rate.

For the last thirty-one years, I've lived within 500 yards of where we're sitting now. I live sixty-five miles from my birthplace. I was not an adventurous child. I was not someone always out there climbing and fording the river, taking Outward Bound programs, the junior varsity football team. I was the child who stayed home, read and wrote, drew pictures and listened to the grownups. Then I got to go to a war that in many ways was even more challenging than the war that Hemingway, William Styron, and James Jones got to go to. I was a whole army that the war was declared against. The cancer was out to get me and nobody else. So I learned things, acquired skills that I wouldn't have dreamed of acquiring otherwise; there's not one of those things that I learned or skills that I would like to rid myself of. If you asked me if I could cancel the quotient of pain I'm in constantly, I would say, "Sure, take it away." If you came in and said, "I can touch your knee and make you stand up and walk," I'd say, "Please do." But if you said, "I can roll the clock back five years and take away everything that's happened since June 1984," I'm not at all certain I'd tell you to do that. It's been a very rich five years. So much has happened; it was quite a ride.

■

HOWIE SEAGO AND LORI SEAGO

I first became aware of Howie Seago when I read a review praising him for his performance in the lead role of Ajax at the Kennedy Center in Washington, D.C. Sometime later I interviewed him in California, where he works and lives. Although he can lipread and speak, Howie prefers to communicate through sign language. His wife and son, who are hearing, are completely conversant in sign language, which gives them a foothold in both worlds. On the occasion of my interview with him, Howie sat opposite me and read my lips as I questioned him. He is an inspiration to talk to—very involved with the deaf community. He works tirelessly to create more opportunities in the arts, particularly the theater, for people who are deaf. His interest in Very Special Arts and its programs led him to join its board of directors.

Howie Seago:

One disadvantage when I was a kid was that my hearing aid would make noises when we'd play war. *Click!* They would always catch me. We'd hide in the forest, but everyone could hear my hearing aid. I should have left it in one place—let it make the noise—and hide somewhere else! I didn't think of that.

It was a family condition. I have an older brother who is hearing impaired. My father is also hard of hearing. Also some of the relatives. So my mother was on the watch for that problem. When it turned up, she sent me to handicapped school right away.

My father didn't even know he had a hearing loss until he was twenty-two. He was in the air force; he'd applied to become a pilot. They said, "You don't qualify because of your hearing loss." He was surprised. They said, "You need a hearing aid." That he hadn't noticed was kind of unusual, since he does have two brothers who have hearing losses, too. About that time they all woke up to the fact that they had hearing losses and needed hearing aids.

My parents were not oversolicitous about whether I was included in the day-to-day life. They didn't make a special effort. I mean, they would repeat things for me sometimes. If someone was talking about something related to me, then they would make sure I understood. Often I would just get a summary, or a synopsis. Watching TV programs, I'd ask my sister, poke her and say, "What'd he say? What'd he say?"

"Shut up—I'll tell you at the commercial!"

Then when the commercial happened, she'd get up and run to the kitchen to get something to eat. Sometimes when she *did* tell me what was going on, I'd think, "Oh, how boring!" My guess of what was going on was often really better than what was *actually* going on.

Many times I felt left out at the dinner table because I couldn't follow the group conversation. I would do fine on a one-to-one basis with my family, but in the group—the family dinners—I was lost. I would always talk with my younger brother, who was also deaf. We had our own homemade sign language. There are three boys in the family, including myself, all with hearing losses. The two girls have none. We have a long-standing joke that they're deaf when they want to be.

Of course, I did have a lot of social problems, especially outside the family. I remember going to dances in junior high school.

Because my father is a Southern Baptist minister, and is against dancing, it was a long time before we could convince him to let us go. I remember being a pretty good dancer—all the girls thought so. But it was hard to get up the nerve to ask a girl to dance. Most of the time they would, but I'd always wonder, "Are they dancing with me because they feel sorry for me, or because they like me?" I guess that's a typical feeling of adolescence—never sure what the real reason is.

I can remember having one girl break up with me in high school because she was afraid of becoming too seriously involved. She couldn't handle the idea of going with a deaf man—or marrying a deaf man and having children who might be deaf. So she thought it was better just to stop before it got too serious. I remember being very upset about that. Very humiliated.

So I had a lot of personal anxiety. Also, there weren't any deaf adult role models really when I was growing up. It was a help to me, of course, that I did have my two brothers who had the same problem. I've always looked up to my older brother. He always did very well—he was a high achiever. I looked up to him, and I think that rubbed off on me: To aim for the best, do the best I can. And having my younger brother gave me a chance to confide in him. And also my family never made me feel bad about being deaf. They always loved me; it didn't matter what.

In college I had a deaf roommate who was interested in theater. He asked me to be in a play. I didn't know sign language very well at that time. I relied on lipreading and a hearing aid. "Don't worry about it," he said. "I'll teach you. Memorize your lines, practice, and you'll do fine." It was a play from the Theater of the Absurd, called *The Feast*. I played the role of an angry young man, very apropos for me at the time because in college I was kind of floundering. I enjoyed the experience. Deaf people came up to me after the show and congratulated me on a wonderful performance. I had to tell them to slow down their signs because I couldn't understand them very well. They were amazed to discover that I was not a fluent signer.

My third year in college, I started a theater company. I thought there'd be something substantial in that, that I could make a positive impact on people, both hearing and deaf. We made a special effort to go to the deaf programs, but we also performed at schools that had no deaf kids in the audience. The idea was not so much to make them aware of the problems of the deaf, but to make them realize that deaf people were interesting, capable, and very likable. We wanted to come on as funny, witty, flashing, charming—so the audience wouldn't see us and just think all deaf are very sullen like in *Johnny Belinda*. Deaf and dumb. Deaf-mute. That kind of image. We wanted to approach it in a different way and change that stereotype.

At the schools where we performed, there were always questions. A lot of students would ask me if deaf people can drive—a real old stereotypical question. I would always answer them in a kind of sarcastic way—"Oh, very carefully! We take our key out of our pocket, we open the door, we put the key in the ignition, put our seat belts on, check our rear-view mirrors, and then we say a prayer!"

They'd ask if we have girlfriends. "Are your girlfriends deaf?"

"No, my girlfriend's hearing."

"So how do you do that?"

"Well, wouldn't you like to know!"

In fact, the power and the magic of sign language will do wonders. Deaf students who grow up in oral programs eventually do learn sign language. It's so much easier to communicate. They can talk about more substantial issues, relevant things, rather than focus all their energies in trying to understand what is being said. My advice for people who want to learn sign language—find a deaf lover. That's how my wife learned.

Lori Seago:

I met Howie in a sign-language class. He was the teacher's aide, and I was a student. I had seen interpreters and thought it was fascinating. So I thought, "Well, why not learn?" So I took a sign-language class. I really enjoyed it. So I took another one and enjoyed it more because Howie was there. And that was it. That's how we met.

Howie Seago:

Because of my work with the children's theater touring company, the college asked me to teach a class that was an introduction to deaf theater. So I taught it during my senior year. After I graduated, I became a consultant for the State of Washington— traveling, doing a one-man show, and giving workshops in creative drama in schools around the state. I did that for about a year. Then I got an offer to go to San Francisco to work on a TV program for deaf children for PBS. It was called *Rainbow's End.* We wrote the scripts, directed, acted—did everything. Made the coffee. The program is no longer around today, unfortunately. It was very hard to attract funding. But it was successful in that it did make a lot of deaf children happy. It woke them up to the fact that there were deaf people outside of their classroom. They enjoyed the show not only because most of the adult performers were deaf, but because we had a couple of deaf children. They were surprised to see deaf children acting.

Most of those kids were in mainstreamed programs without any interaction with deaf kids outside their own school. I think that's the big problem with mainstreaming today—the problem of isolation, with just a very limited interaction with the world. Their education suffers. Most of the time the interpreters are not well trained. Often they are high school students who maybe have taken one or two sign-language classes. And that's not appropriate. Interpreters who do become fairly good will move on to the college level—they won't stay in the high school, or elementary or junior high. The answer is that they should have a center, and bus the kids from all around the city to that one central location where they would have several really accomplished deaf teachers and a lot more resources to work with.

And also what is needed is more of the arts in the classroom, in any form, whether it's drama, dance, painting, pottery, whatever. Give the deaf children a creative outlet. Because they do have a lot of frustration and anger that comes from the feeling of not being able to communicate fluently.

In my case, my parents taught me. Also, I went to an oral program that taught me how to speak. Now I feel that there was too much emphasis on the oral training in my life, and not enough on the educational aspects. I would have liked to have learned more about history, geography, and all that, instead of the emphasis on speech.

As for speaking, nobody really knows what is involved in helping a deaf child speak. Many hearing-impaired people who have a very slight hearing loss may not be able to learn to speak as well as some deaf people who have a profound hearing loss. It's very odd. My hearing loss—according to general patterns—is such that I shouldn't be able to speak as well as I do.

Sign language, though, is the key. The other day I watched a videotape of a woman telling a story in sign language, talking about when she was little and about her interaction with her mother. I enjoyed it so much. It was just a pleasure to watch someone telling a great story in a language that I could understand. I didn't have to work double time, my mind busy trying to decipher what she was saying—the language mode, the English, or whatever—by lipreading.

I'm a better than average lip-reader myself. My language, my vocabulary, is very good, and I read very well. But still, it's impossible for anyone to lipread completely. Word for word. For myself, I can catch maybe 75 percent of what you're saying on a one-to-one. And even that is a struggle. I have to know the framework of what we're talking about and be able to understand your lip movements. So many different people have different mouth structures.

Actually I can hear voices and sounds, but I can't filter out the noise from the voices. So being able to hear vaguely doesn't really help, though in a quiet room, it does help a lot. It also helps me to monitor my voice, if I'm talking too loud, or not loud enough. I drive my wife crazy with the feedback from my hearing aids— they whistle.

We're often asked whether we think being deaf is the most difficult of all the handicaps, because of the silence—being really in silence. True, communication is cut off. But I'm not sure it's the most difficult of all handicaps. What about the person who has cerebral palsy or someone who's in a wheelchair? Still, one way to cut through the silence is through the arts. If the schools could take advantage of deaf people who are in the community—bring them in to share their artistic talents, bring in deaf adults to tell stories about what it was like in the old days when they were deaf, or just to tell any stories—it would be wonderful and thrilling, a treat for the deaf kids to see a deaf grandpa telling a story in his own special, colorful way. Different than a hearing teacher who's signing in the classroom.

A lot of people say there's sort of a deaf culture. I don't blame them. I respect it. The deaf culture is important to me, too. It's a place where I feel I belong. We all have to have something we feel we belong to—our own family, our neighborhood, whatever. We need a place where I'm one of other people who are all alike. Actually, a lot of hearing people come into the deaf world. Some come in for the wrong reasons, perhaps because they're a failure in their own world, not able to achieve, or attain a leadership position. So they think, "Oh, I'll become a leader among deaf people." Not *all* of them are like that, but we've come across a few whose motives are not exactly all that altruistic!

Lori Seago:

We're very happy. Marriages that fail between deaf and hearing people tend to be because of communication—the hearing person may not be fluent enough in sign language. They have problems. So would I. If I want to go to a party with all hearing people, then what is my role? Am I there as a person who's participating in the party? Or am I there only to interpret for my husband? We don't go to a lot of those parties because of that. It makes it easier for both of us to select the parties that have some deaf people there, or people who know sign language. We've kind of altered our lifestyle to satisfy the needs of both of us.

Howie Seago:

I have friends with hearing spouses, some with deaf spouses. I do find that I identify a little bit more with those who have hearing spouses, because my own wife is hearing.

Our son, who is two, signs. He talks a lot. He learned how to sign before he learned how to talk. That's our strong belief—that sign language should be used from the day of birth for a deaf child. The problem is parents don't know if they have a deaf child until the child is older—maybe six months, one year old, two years—sometimes five years old. Then they find out. I believe that sign language should be used from the beginning to help facilitate the language processing—the mechanism in the mind for the language development. I look at my son, and I can see that his mind is really working, figuring out things. I wasn't afraid that he might have a hearing problem at all. In fact, I always thought my child would be deaf, because of all the boys in my family who are.

Lori Seago:

I didn't really care because, again, you know, we were prepared for it. It didn't really bother me. People will think, "Oh, my gosh!"—but actually we were a little disappointed! "Oh, he's hearing?" I mean, we're totally happy with him, and we have no regrets, but there's something a little special about carrying on a tradition. I mean, they're unique, and we wanted to show people that—it's okay, you know? But we're happy that he's hearing.

Howie Seago:

We're thinking about adopting a deaf child, later maybe. If we can find one.

I'm very proud of what I'm doing now, today. It gives me a wide range of perspectives on life—to get into the mind of different kinds of people, people who are different from myself. A military man, a clown, a beast. But if I didn't have my sign-language skills today, I wouldn't be an actor. There's no way that I can speak like a hearing person on stage. I can't. I would be reduced to being a spear carrier or a waiter, that's all. But because of my sign-language ability—the power and magic of sign language—I can make the words come alive and larger on stage.

What happens when we perform is that the other actors speak for me on stage. I sign. People find that very dynamic. Because of my signs, my characters really expand. In *Ajax,* people thought that I was six five—or seven feet tall! The stage was set at an angle, so I looked huge, but my signs made me look even larger!

Almost any play with a surreal theme of magical elements can accommodate a deaf actor without sacrificing too much of the author's original intentions. For example, in the La Jolla production of *The Tempest,* we had Ariel provide some vocal narration for my portrayal of Caliban. I don't think Shakespeare would have minded!

In our production of *Beauty and the Beast,* which was put on by the Honolulu Theatre for Youth, we had the character of Beauty learn and use sign language during the course of the play as a symbolic indication of her trust and fondness for the Beast. The Beast signs his lines with a vocal narration provided by a shadowy figure in black onstage . . . which added to the element of mystery in the play. In fact, we suggested that this character was involved in the curse that transformed the prince into a beast. At the end of the play, when the Beast is transformed back into the Prince, we cut out the speaking lines entirely, leaving them to sign—a visually stunning interlude with the lovers stepping up the grand staircase to a large, stained-glass window. Violins! The works!

■

ALISON SHEEN

Several years ago I visited the Very Special Arts
New Visions Dance Project, which was being
conducted in London under the auspices of the
Royal Ballet. A young blind woman was partic-
ipating in the class. I noticed her immediately.
Her movements were exquisite. She had a grace
and ease about her that was quite extraordi-
nary, particularly for someone who was blind.
I asked if she would be willing to be inter-
viewed for this book. She agreed and later ar-
rived at my hotel, to which she came by
underground, alone, using a cane. We had tea
together. She left me with the strong feeling
that all things are possible.

I spent most of my time with the dog in the woods, climbing
trees and exploring. My mother thought ballet might be a good
idea. I quite enjoyed it. I stayed in ballet classes for six years. Then
I went horse-mad as a lot of young girls do. My parents couldn't
afford to let me do both. I had to choose one or the other. I didn't
hesitate. I chose horses. I still like horses, but I don't ride now. I
used to ride when I lived in Devon, because there're no trees out

on the moors. But here in London, if you want to ride, they say, "Well, for you we've got a disabled class on such and such a day."

Well, I'm *not* disabled. I can ride a horse; I just can't see. I don't want to go out with the disabled class. I want to go out with a seeing person who can take me galloping. I've got a good seat, I know how to stay on the horse.

I started to lose my sight in late 1980. From being able to see properly, it took about six months for it to get to the stage it's at now. Which is quite quick, although being in a car accident and losing it overnight might be much more traumatic. It came upon me in the last part of 1980—glaucoma. I was married to somebody sighted. But the marriage wasn't too good, and this just about finished it off. So I had to leave my house, my job, my husband—everything—all within about nine months. My husband just didn't take it seriously. He refused to believe that my sight was going. Actually, he'd met somebody else, anyway, and he was more interested in setting up with that person. I knew the marriage would break up eventually. This just happened to make it speedier.

You think at the time, "I'm never going to be able to cope with this. Too many things are happening. How much can human emotions take?" But in a way it's a good thing it happens so quickly. Then you can start all over again all at once . . . a new lifestyle.

From the age of seven until I was eighteen, I had attacks of blindness; but they cleared and after three weeks I had normal vision again. When I was twenty-two I had another attack. Then I started to get a cataract in one eye. They gave me contact lenses, But then the other eye started to go, so they operated on that one for cataracts. I must have been thirty at the time.

Right before I left the hospital the doctor did a very thorough examination. By putting some kind of mirror into my eye, he had a good look around. He informed me that I was at the very early stages of glaucoma. I remember not wanting to talk to anybody. I just lay in the hospital bed crying. I was really upset because I knew what it meant. I had seen other people with glaucoma and what it had done to their eyes: The disease made their eyes slitted and pink—closed up, very peculiar. Mine aren't like that, I've been told. I'm very lucky. But part of my despair came from vanity, and also, of course, because I was going to lose my sight. Old ladies had glaucoma. Older people. Not someone thirty!

At the time the doctor said he could do something about it— they had plenty of treatments and they were going to start right away. I can't fault him. I was with him for ten years and I thought he was marvelous. He tried every drop he could, every tablet, even an operation in the end, but nothing could stop it. I was one of those people where it couldn't be stopped. They can catch it in some people, but I was nonresponsive. The operation was done in Cambridge. It worked to a certain extent. I can tell the difference between night and day, light or dark, in one eye. Psychologically that is very helpful.

I wasn't actually told that I would lose my eyesight. I think that my surgeon, on purpose, did not mention this. He's a bit of a psychologist, as well as being an eye surgeon. I think he thought I'd go to pieces if I was actually told. He wasn't going to destroy me in one second by telling me.

The worst is waking up every morning while your sight is going and thinking—shall I open my eyes or not? Will it be gone? Will I be able to see perfectly again? And you keep them shut as long as you possibly can until it's time to get up. When you open them, the disappointment is tremendous. Because you can only see as well as you did the day before. Or even less, maybe.

Mother took it worst of all, because she's a bit of a fusspot anyway. She was very upset and got to the stage where she wanted me to sleep in her bed with her, which I did for about three days. But it wasn't really helping. She was too sympathetic. I began shouting at her, and it just got beyond being anything reasonable. She said I could come and live with her. I said, "Well, thank you." It would have been the absolute last resort . . . I'd prefer being destitute. Nothing against her, but I knew it would be the end of me if I moved in with her. So I moved to the Midlands—with a friend of mine.

You get to know your home. In the home you do fine. I had a telemobility officer right away to help me learn cane technique.

She took me everywhere, practicing. She took me to a school on holidays when it was empty. She took me on the train, on the street, to the shops. A mobility officer's got to be satisfied that you can use the white cane properly before they let you have one. Every time she took me home from mobility lessons with the white cane, she took the cane away with her. I wasn't ready—too much of a danger to myself and everyone else. It's still difficult. I don't go very fast. I'm a plodder; my pace isn't as fast as other blind people.

My friends didn't make any allowances for me. It was upsetting for them, which I didn't realize at the time. They kept it a good secret. When I went to live with them, they didn't move anything. The only thing they did was give me a specially marked measuring cup for the milk.

I cooked the dinner while they were out at work. It's not that difficult. How much is involved in peeling a potato? How much do you look when you're chopping something? It's kind of automatic. It's slower for me, but not very hard. The only problem is carving. I can cut a slice of cake or bread, but I can't carve. Cooking is something that's never really bothered me, though I do worry about the gas stove.

I was hairdressing at the time I was diagnosed. I was about to take my horse-riding examination so I could teach riding. I had to stop everything. I noticed that certain friends—especially male friends—couldn't take it. Because I was so active as a sighted person, I think it really upset some of them. I've never seen them again . . . never heard from them again. In the Midlands it was better. My two closest friends from there are still just the same. They didn't make any allowances. I was always expected to go with them. I was never asked, "Are you coming along?" You were *dragged* along, and that was it. So I had a good start in that respect—I was never left out of anything. I never felt lonely.

When I moved out from my friends, I was terribly depressed for a year or more. I had a lodger, who was a friend, but I'd sit home alone. I tried to join evening classes and get enthusiastic. But it just didn't come. I went along for the sake of it. I must have had the same dreary look on my face all the time. I was totally unmotivated—lethargic, apathetic. Weekends didn't mean anything, it was just one day after another. Then I met somebody at one of the classes who was interested in politics. It was what's called a transactional analysis class—which is about being aware of how you're going to deal with a situation before it happens without getting into a dither.

In 1982—about a year later—I went to this center in Torbay. It's in Devon. That was the worst time—the rehabilitation center. They were teaching me things like how to use a washing machine. I told them, "This is a waste of time. Teach someone who doesn't know how to use a washing machine." I'd been using a washing machine since I lost my sight, cooking and cleaning, and so forth. Really, you don't look at that sort of thing when you do it sighted too much, do you? It's automatic and boring. I stopped it after the first lesson. I said, "I'd like to be doing Braille, please, instead." So they put me in Braille class. It took me two years to learn it properly. I kept putting it down and leaving it and then picking it up again.

I'm very proud of that, actually. I think, "I really know how to do this!" I don't *like* it. But I just think it's so incredible to have learned how to do it. Now I read with no concentration of any sort. I also learned to use an Opticon. In one hand you hold a small camera with a very small lens which will scan one letter at a time, moving it down the page, line by line. With your index finger on your left hand, you feel a little pad that's got about 120 pins in it. As the camera shines on the letter—say the letter *N*—it will bring up the pins in the shape of an *N* into your finger. It's the proper alphabet—alphabet-shaped under your finger. I recommend it. For anybody who was able to read print at one time who's lost their sight, I recommend that, rather than Braille; they'll feel more at home.

I remarried in 1985. I gave myself a nice long time—about four years—having boyfriends and doing the same as everybody else does, you know. My husband is partially sighted. I couldn't stand John at first! I thought he was a know-it-all. I said, to my friend Sheila, "Who is that person? He's a real pain."

He had resigned from his job, and taken a job at the hostel

where I was staying, serving meals, being a night watchman until he could find another job. I thought, then, that he had a nice voice. A low voice with a slight northern accent.

John belongs to a drama group. He came home one night and said to me, "I think you ought to go to the next workshop at the drama group because they've got a dance teacher taking it." I had danced as a child. I'd been in a couple of local talent shows. At the age of twenty-five, I took up dancing again, and I started tap, which I'd never done before. I was getting on quite well with that when the glaucoma started; it was the end of everything for me. I threw the tap shoes in the dustbin—everything—photographs, all sorts of things that I couldn't look at, which I regret now. I was angry. Furious. It can't have been anything else.

So when my husband suggested the dance workshop, I said, "Oh, that's good—I'll go along." That's where I met Wolfgang Steiner for the first time. Afterward he said to me, "Would you like to come along to my Monday dance class?" He more or less invites people. So I said yes. I didn't go until the following June, when I got a friend to come with me. I enjoyed it, because I found I was able to let my frustrations out. I can't walk along very quickly, but in there I can run around—especially if someone's got my hand—and it gets rid of all that frustration.

You must attempt things you'd never dream of doing when you were sighted. You must take the opportunity. Because so many things can happen. You reach people who can introduce you to something further on again. You don't know who you're going to bump into. So it's best to actually take part. Even if nothing happens, it's no loss. I was afraid, at one time, of making a fool of myself. But I've got to the stage where I don't care. I can't see people looking at me. So it doesn't matter.

I belong to two classes. I go by myself to Covent Garden—Stanley Hamilton's classes. He's the main teacher of dancing in Very Special Arts. I go to his class on Monday nights. It starts at 5:30 and it ends at 7:00 P.M. Coming back we all walk down to the station together for safety, and then we all split up and go our separate ways.

The other classes are at Barons Court. Because it's such a

horrible road to cross, with parked cars and bicycles everywhere, I normally meet one of the girls before the class. We walk up to the church.

If I had never danced before, it would have been more difficult. It's odd: Others are partially sighted, but they haven't danced before, so they get a bit confused. I've danced before, but I can't see at all, so I get confused. So really we're all on the same level. We have a mixed class. There are able-bodied but blind people, mentally handicapped, and psychologically handicapped people who've had some trauma and not quite gotten over it. You have to be invited to join, because Wolfgang can only cope with so many at a time. There can be as many as thirty-six. They always come regularly when there's rehearsal for a show. But when it's just classes, people may drop out for a couple of weeks because they've got other things to do. But you're always welcomed back again. He'll say, "Oh, *there* you are—you weren't here last week."

It's good to actually commit yourself to something. One week we had to practice a dance—six of us. Everybody else seemed to know what to do because they'd done it before. I didn't know it very well, and I sprained a muscle in my hip. He got a bottle of whiskey and paper cups, and we all had a cup each—just about three swigs for each. Everybody was *wonderful* out on the floor after that! He's the kind of man who will take advantage to be creative with anything he can find. Somebody brought a baby in once; he was handing it round, saying, "We must do this like the baby's doing—we've got to hold her hand like the baby's doing." The baby loved it! Everybody lets Wolfgang do as he pleases, because we trust him.

We've just came back from Dublin, where we were Irish peasants doing village dances. There were two groups, A and B, made up of blind and partially blind. What is difficult is the distancing—running toward a group and actually knowing where they are without crashing into them. They pound their feet just beforehand, so we can get a sense of where they are. We have clues like that; it's not a question of just wildly running around.

When you reach the other group, touch is all important to tell you where you are and prevent you from wandering into the audience. You can actually work it out so that you get help, a hand touching yours, though it doesn't look like it. It looks like part of the dance.

It's an extraordinary experience. I do believe in the spiritual: some kind of force—the earth, the elements, whatever, something nearer to nature. I feel energy from people. That's what I feel in these classes—a lot of energy going between us, through arms, heads, feet. I'm not a religious person at all. From the very beginning, my friends helped me to go on. They wouldn't let me get to the depression stage. When I get approached by people in the street—these sort of devout Christian people—I get a bit annoyed. I'm a sitting target for them. I have no means of walking away if I want to. If they're at the bus stop, I have to put up with them. They say to me, "Oh, don't you believe that God will make you see?" I say, "Well, no, I don't, actually." "Don't you believe in anything?" I say, "Yes, I believe in my friends and myself." They think I'm a real heathen.

Some people are a nuisance to blind people, especially if they're drunk. But then you can get run over quite easily without the help of a drunkard. Some people, of course, are very perceptive. They'll see you heading for the station just off line, so they just pull you over a tiny bit without saying anything. Somebody else may see you heading toward the escalator, half a foot out, and they'll pull you over to get you in a straight line for it. They say, "Two steps and you're home."

I've got this game I play—to see if I can get home without anybody helping me! It's a bit cruel, because sometimes you really do need people's help. Even if you don't really want to accept it. Some days you just want to amble along just like everybody else—days when you are gritting your teeth because people are coming up to help and you don't want to be bothered. But you have to be nice.

Personally I can't memorize many places. I try. I learn usually with John. He'll take me on a trip, and he'll pick out things I'll need to know—a gap here, a gap there, a rubbish bin here, and then you turn left. I do it with him, because I can get cross and he really doesn't care.

When you can't see people, you tend to listen to them more. You give them the opportunity to get their point over to you. People who can see take one look at a person and say, "Humph, he's scruffy!" But he might be a very nice person! Because I'm not sighted, I have a chance to find out. There're other compensations.

My family doesn't actually seem to worry about me half as much as they do about my sister, whose traumas are so much more than any of mine. Her car broke down the other day and cost her £600 to mend. That's something else that not being sighted has done for me. A lot of things seem very trivial that might have been like a mountain before I lost my sight.

Touch and hearing are definitely used more now. And, of course, the brain—you've got to have some kind of memory for certain things like journeys. I've found that I can't store too much. Somebody phones up and says, "Oh, can I meet you at such-and-such cottage?" I may have been there once, but I think, "Oh, God—I can't remember." But I'll go there anyway. I can ask somebody the way out and whatever I need to do. I tend to be a bit reckless. I grab the nearest person and I say, "Excuse me, is this so and so?" Quite a few people are used to helping blind people around. You'll get a shoulder tap, they'll turn you a certain way and sort of push you gently along the right direction. They seem to know what they're doing without having to speak to you.

It's probably more difficult for a man, because a man is accustomed to having a lot done for him by a wife, a girlfriend, whomever. He's got to learn from the start how to make a cup of tea. How to boil an egg. Simple things—how to cook potatoes. A woman knows all these things by a certain age. But there's no way of getting away from the depression. You've got to go through that to come out the other side. No matter what I say to them, they'll think it will never be the same again. Well, it won't be quite the same, but you might find it a new kind of richness.

Obviously, I'd like to have my sight back tomorrow, but I wouldn't want anything to change about my attitude toward people. That would frighten me—and I'd feel sad, if it changed for the worse.

The basic thing I tell everybody who says, "Aren't you brave!"

is, "Well, you've got two choices. Either you stay in and vegetate, or you frighten yourself to death and go out with a cane or dog or whatever—you know, for the first time—and after a while it's not so frightening. And then you start to live a bit." What is it in a person—an ordinary person, any person—that makes them go on? You can read a book about heroes, but it's hard for people to relate to them sometimes. "Well, they can do that, but I'm not that . . . I'm a schoolteacher. I'm not some great ballet dancer who's been paralyzed." So that's what it is. We are ordinary people whose lives changed in some way.

■

RANDY SOUDERS

Randy, who lives in Fort Worth, Texas, is a successful artist who serves on the board of Very Special Arts; he uses a wheelchair. I interviewed Randy at the International Very Special Arts Festival in Washington, D.C., where he conducted workshops in painting. He has an extremely positive outlook on life, loves his work, and is altogether a joy to be with.

Just prior to my accident I was a pretty typical seventeen-year-old. I had a strong interest in doing something artistic because I'd had a knack for drawing and painting, drawn to it from an early age. I was planning a commercial career—in graphic design, advertising illustration, something like that, because I saw that this might be a way I could actually make a living. Artists, unfortunately, so often have the prefix of "starving" before "artist."

Then, that Saturday. My best friend, my younger cousin, and I decided to go up to a local lake and cool off. Texas summers are notoriously scorchers. So we went out to this old swimming hole, and I just dove in. I hit something under the water. To this day I don't know what it was, because it was a fairly deep hole, perhaps a log floating around just under the water. Whatever it was, I hit it head-on and suffered a compression-type injury—broke a couple of vertebrae in my neck and badly jammed my spinal cord. My friends were still on the edge of the water waiting for me to reappear. You know, kids will dive in and stay under for a long time, just to pretend they're not coming up. Well, my friends eventually got the idea—hey, he's *not* coming up. So they went in and fished me out, floated me over to the edge—to a little sandy area—and left me half-in, half-out of the water. They knew it was serious. They didn't try to pick me up or move me; they ran and called an ambulance. The ambulance people came and secured me to a board and took me out that way.

Afterward, there was as much emotional trauma as physical for me, because on the other side I had been completely physical, athletic, whatever, and it was almost like being ripped from one body, one that worked, and placed in another one that didn't—just that quick. Instantly, I couldn't do anything.

For five months I was in this hospital, feeling such a useless burden, not only to family, but friends and society. The bills piled up unbelievably.

And, too, your self-image is just instantly altered. You're relabeled with terms like "handicapped" or "quadriplegic," "crippled," or—I love this one, "invalid"—you know, "in-valid." These labels all conjured up a new self-image of helplessness, dependency, and worth*less*ness, just being *less* than others. Hospitals to me weren't dull places; there was plenty of activity going on. But you just felt so helpless. They come and get you; they wheel you down here, and they do this to you. You're really not in charge of anything.

Everyone, I guess, has this feeling of "Why me?" But all in all, I look back, and I think, "Well, why *not* me?" What happened to me happens so many thousands of times each year—especially to young athletic males who are out there playing games, jumping off things, riding bikes and motorcycles. Every year the hospitals fill up with these young boys who've taken a bad spill. Yeah. I felt the anger, the depression. I don't think I ever got to that point where I wanted to end it all. But I was just so—fed up. After you fail at some minor little task so many times, you are just exasperated—dropping something on the floor, and trying to get it back up again. You get frustrated to the point of wanting to scream.

I never was in pain, really. It was like a big spring had snapped inside me. It's really quite an incomplete injury. I cannot walk, but I've got feeling, to some degree, pretty much all over. I've got movement in my right leg and grip in my right hand.

Then near the end of my stay in the hospital one of my therapists almost forcibly strapped a paintbrush to my hand. I was encouraged to paint. The therapists had seen some of the things I'd done prior to my injury. Being reluctant—not wanting to fail again at something, not wanting to see how bad it could be—I was pleasantly surprised at the result. I found that I still had this tiny little spark of artistic ability left. So it was almost like a big weight had been lifted off. I immediately started fueling and fanning that spark until I had a little flame. I still think that flame has provided the light I needed to see my way out of this forest. At least I could do something worthwhile again, and it was, I think, a vital part of my recovery.

Unfortunately, I'm left-handed, and that affects me when it comes to painting because I have no finger movement or grip at all in my left hand. That's the hand I have to paint with. I tried my right, and it just never would work. That's pretty significant because it almost forces me to be a painter, rather than, for example, an illustrator. I need a frictionless kind of medium, one onto which the paint flows smoothly and fairly effortlessly, because I have very little strength. I have big trouble signing credit-card slips, because you've got to go through three or four sheets of carbon paper. I have to sign them individually. If I try to apply pressure, the pen just pops out of my hand.

When I left the hospital, I stayed at home. I didn't go out. I was embarrassed. I preferred being a recluse and painting in seclusion. That's where a lot of my early work stemmed from—just being cloistered away, working like a monk. I turned out a sizable volume of things in those earlier days. Being introspective helped me artistically. But socially I found that I cut myself off from society. And it's important not to do that. No one can get along in this world without love and acceptance, and I'm not different. In fact, that may be the main reason I do what I do, because I get such gratification from people I don't know who come up, elated to meet me because of what I do or who I am. Staying at home, I began to see, was turning into a bad situation, just by my not being out in public—not being active.

So it wasn't that I was forced, but when fall comes along, well, it's time for college. Everyone had been telling me when to get up, when to eat, where to go, and what to do at that point anyway, so I said, "Okay. It's fall. It's time for college." And I started at the University of Texas.

It really was scary at first. Not knowing if you can get around, having to ask total strangers for help, getting those first looks and stares and what-all. Dealing with things like opening doors and getting up little hills. The deep-piled carpet is a menace to society! Rolling around in a wheelchair, it just bogs you down. Sometimes a little step an inch high is as much as a mile; you just can't get over it.

The last two years I lived in a dormitory. There was a program for disabled students organized by the Texas Rehabilitation Commission that arranged for assistance if you needed it, or anything it took to get you an education. Among other things, these programs arrange for a student to participate as an aide to another student, for which they get some financial assistance, their room free or something. It's like having a job on campus. I was quite independent compared to some of the others. A young boy across the hall was pretty far along with muscular dystrophy, very dependent on assistance, getting in and out of bed, everything. To help me, I had a former helicopter pilot for the South Vietnamese Army. He flew one of those giant Chinook copters. He had been evacuated, and he was at the university getting an economics degree. It was great having him as a roommate because he was nice and quiet, and very studious.

In college I majored in advertising art—graphics, graphic design. From college I went right into an internship at an ad agency. I was there about three months. I happened to have one of my paintings leaning up along the wall to be photographed by our staff photographer. The director of one of the banks we had been doing work for saw it, and started commenting on how much he liked it. He asked if I had more; did I ever do art shows.

So I was given an exhibition. Much to my surprise, I found that people liked the stuff and would pay hard-earned money for it. That was about eleven years ago. When I sold paintings, I would take what I made and reinvest it into my little operation of creating and making prints. It took a long time to get going. It's sort of like towing a battleship. It takes a lot of energy to get it moving, but then after a while it sort of has its own momentum; you just have to fuel it a bit. Now I've got six employees in my office. We distribute prints and posters of the paintings. It's through distribution that things really mushroom in a hurry. Fifteen hundred galleries have carried my work at one time or another. Right now I've got around 25,000 individual collectors on my computer. So when I release a new print, it's like having this big dry sponge out there soaking up a goodly portion of them, and very quickly. I try to keep my prints very accessible. The average is in the $30 to $50 range for something that's signed and not a limited edition. Twenty-two or twenty-three limited editions have sold out. Supply and demand takes over.

It was the art that provided the motivation for me to get up every morning and do something instead of sitting in front of the TV. It's very easy to get sucked into a dependency routine—you know, this "give me, give me, give me" kind of attitude. Society has such diminished expectations of the disabled person. It doesn't expect you to be able to do much of anything. It under-challenges us to perform on a par with them. And that's what I take most pride in—the fact that what I'm doing today is well received all over, even with people who haven't a clue as to my physical condition. Then, when they learn about the paralysis and the story behind it, their mouths just drop and hang open. The gallery owners, for example, are flabbergasted that I can do any-thing. So that's what I take some measure of pride in: They don't say, "Gee, this is good, considering your condition . . . blah, blah, blah." They say, "Boy, this is good, *period*." And they dig in their wallets and pull out the money. That, for me, is a kick.

The first impression when you roll in in a wheelchair says loud and clear: "Hey, this guy has a problem of some sort. Gee, he must be sick!" Or whatever. Disabled means un-abled. Kids, on the other hand, are great! They come running right up and ask, point-blank, "Why are you in that wheelchair?" Their parents get red as beets, apologize, and back off. I have seen that again and again. They sort of jerk the kid's arm, "Don't, don't, don't."

And that's really a shame. I wish I had a little comic book to give to these kids that explains what disabled people are all about—whatever is wrong with them, whether they need wheelchairs or are blind or can't hear—so that a parent could read the book to them, not only for the kids but for *them*, so that they can answer these questions and form attitudes at an early age. Because when a kid is reprimanded for being inquisitive, I think he instantly gets a feeling of—whoops!—there's something wrong here.

Since society has diminished expectations of us, that we're really not expected to do a whole lot, once you show them otherwise, it helps the average person to see that "maybe these folks are really capable of doing a lot more than I thought."

The last thing on my mind when I get up every morning is that I'm in a wheelchair. I mean, it is the *very* last thing on my list. I get up. I've got so much going on, if I want to go someplace I just get up and go. Of course, my condition does mean that I have to plan my days. If I know I need to go to a certain place, I've got to think, "Gee, can I get in there when I get there? Or can I park when I get there?" If I'm by myself, I've got to deal with the accessibility problems that have been around forever. So those things do creep in. Or, if you're going to be out for an evening, you want to know if there's a bathroom that you can get to. Those things are real questions. But other than that, I am not at all hesitant to get out in the middle of things. It's just not a problem anymore.

I enjoy traveling. I have a van that's equipped with just about everything I need. It's almost a land yacht. It has the hand controls and a lift—power seats. It converts into a sleeper in the back if I'm tired. The hand controls are ingenious. They hook onto the accelerator and the brake, and I just pull this knob down to accelerate, and push it to stop—it's that simple. I can accelerate and brake with one hand, and steer with the other. They put one of these little spinner knobs on your steering wheel that are illegal in most states (because they want people to use two hands), but they are legal for anyone using hand controls.

It's odd. If I had a crystal ball to see what would have happened had I not had the injury, I don't see myself having done what I've done at all. I would probably have a mediocre position in a mediocre little ad agency and be like the rest of society—up to my ears in debt, just trying to get by—and being frustrated that I didn't go for something that would have truly inspired me all along. I would probably—knowing me—have gotten crazy about some girl, gotten married, just all the typical things. I don't know that I would have dedicated myself to art. Art was a vital part of my recovery from my injury. I found myself in a situation of being the same person in a new body, one that didn't work, along with the loss of self-esteem and self-confidence and all the things that come along with a traumatic injury. Once I realized that I still had a chance at being creative and of value through my artwork, I just really focused in on that. It was a real part of my recovery. The accident almost forced me to be focused. You become locked into a positive type of prison in which you are able to function on your own. I have a home studio that I paint in, which is separate from my gallery and frame-shop business. It's quiet here all the time. I can paint into the night or early in the morning—whenever I feel like it. I've painted on Thanksgiving and even at Christmas, because I enjoy painting.

Of course, there are some things that I wish could have changed. Initially, everyone rallies around you, you know—they're supportive. All the friends I had at the time of the accident were right there—right from the beginning. Then, as time went on, one by one they kind of drifted away, slowly. I think it was because they obviously didn't know how to react to me—and I certainly didn't know how to make things easier on them. I was having a hard enough time trying to figure out what was happening to me. I don't know if I pushed them away or if they felt that

I wasn't the same person. It was a very gradual thing, but most of them just kind of drifted off. And I drifted off into myself.

These days it's different. My new friends know me and like me—wheelchair and all—and the common thing is they say (and this happened just the other night): "I don't even see your chair. I don't see you being the least bit disabled." It wasn't a factor; it wasn't an issue. Who would have thought? It's not as big a deal as people make it out. My disability is a little more obvious than others, but it's all in the eye of the beholder. I have great vision; yet I have friends who can't see anything without their glasses. But I'm the one who is labeled disabled. It may be just that mine is more the stereotypical view of disability.

At the early stage, you really can't see how you can do it. Because so many things are closed to you or they're being done for you, and you have bad dreams of what life' going to be like in the future. So many folks say, "Oh, gee, if this ever happened to me, I don't think I would want to go on. I just wouldn't want to get up every day. I'd just rather end my life." Well, you really can't say things like that until you're in that position. Then you find out you have many other talents and abilities that you didn't realize. Now I'm just about as independent as anybody. It's convenient for me to get others to do the dishes, the laundry and such things. I say, "Listen, I can do this, but I think I'm a little more valuable painting than I am doing housework." So that's often gotten me out of a few chores that I don't exactly like to do. I do just about anything I feel like doing . . . except tap dancing.

Fifty years ago, you had to go out and plow a field or whatever to earn a living. Today we're in an information society. It is not as physically demanding as it used to be, so there's just as much opportunity for disabled people. In a strange way, an injury like this, while it greatly complicates your life, also simplifies it. It complicates some things: like, it takes longer to get dressed; it's a more involved ordeal. But in many ways it's just easier to stay put and get focused on what you're doing. I don't want to squash a kid's dream when he's in a hospital just so sure he's going to tap dance his way out of there in six weeks. But I would want to reassure him by saying that there is a lot of support out there, a lot of help and advice. Whether you're an acrobat leaping around or you're in a wheelchair, you can have a very fulfilling life and really make a difference in this world. As human beings, we are supremely adaptable.

I'm having a good time. That's one of the perks. I'm one of the few guys—artists—that can ask a girl to come up and see my etchings and really make it sound believable.

■

LAUREEN SUMMERS AND EARL SHOOP

Laureen has worked with Very Special Arts for many years—as a member of the staff, an adviser, and currently a member of the board of directors. Although she has had cerebral palsy since birth, and occasionally has some difficulty being understood, Laureen has been a wonderfully effective spokesperson for Very Special Arts and an advocate for people with disabilities. She is remarkably intelligent, works full time, is married, and has a beautiful little girl. Her courage and determination have been an inspiration to me and to all who have met her.

Laureen Summers:

I was born in New York, *conceived* in the Village. I always think that was a romantic beginning. But when I was born, I wasn't breathing, and that resulted in the cerebral palsy . . . the disease that Christy Brown has in the film *My Left Foot,* which won an Academy Award. I loved *My Left Foot.* It's odd. The reviews left one thinking Christy Brown was unable to use his body. Then you go to the movie and you see him hurling himself down the stairs and managing to score field goals. The reviewers kind of got hooked on portraying him as being a victim, rather than having a full life. In terms of cerebral palsy, I thought it was wonderful.

What I hear about cerebral palsy is that if you don't get oxygen within the first six minutes of life, the damage begins to the nervous system, and the neurological process results in the condition. That is what I've been told. No one seems to know. I was taken to doctors. I know my parents were told I would never walk. A cousin of my mother, a doctor in Montreal, figured that I had cerebral palsy when I was six months old. My parents thought the condition would go away. Growing up, I didn't get a lot of information about what was going on with me and my body. It was a long time—maybe into my teens—before I started to figure out what was happening. No one talked about it. My parents never joined a support group, so it was pretty isolating. I remember writing a paper in college on creativity, and that one of the ways creativity is defined is people wanting to change things, or make something different. Sometimes I think my yearning to create began when I discovered I *didn't* know what was going on. So I wanted to change things, and I wanted to see if I could put together pieces of my life. Doesn't that make sense?

I don't remember much about my early childhood. In fourth grade I remember people avoiding me. I always had friends, but with certain people, there was kind of a reluctance to let me come very close. I sensed the discomfort. It was years and years before I could talk about it. When I was twelve and thirteen, walking down the street, people made fun of me. Imitating. It wasn't fun.

My family never made me feel I wouldn't be okay. I felt like I wasn't allowed to talk about it. So that in itself created a lot of conflict. I don't remember having discussions about it, and my parents were afraid to go into it too much, so I was always wondering—there was something going on that I couldn't get in touch with. My mother was afraid to tell me things because I would get upset.

If I could change what I've been through, I would have asked my parents for more information. Things would have been a lot easier. I could have been reassured that my life wasn't in danger. I had no way of knowing that I was secure within my family.

With Melanie, my daughter, I do try to tell her things—reassure her. We make lots of mistakes as parents. My parents were great people, but they were a little scared.

My mother is a violinist and a painter. She both played and painted for many years. When I was very young and we lived in New York, my parents used to have musicians over on Friday nights. My attraction to the arts was always that a lot of the people they associated with were very independent and dynamic and weird—not willing to settle for the conventional—questioning things about the world. So I felt a kind of kinship. So many other people around me seemed to be accepting life without any response. I wanted more than that. Along the way I figured that out: You've got to be powerful enough to make things different.

At a special school in Baltimore [the William S. Berry School] I was drawn to the arts, because it provided a relief, and I could do what I wanted. No one thought I could *do* anything. My one memory is leading a dance in fourth grade; that was my big highlight.

I felt very competitive with my nondisabled peers. But I think it would have been easier if we talked about it. I really had no point of reference. I had a lot of uncomfortable feelings. I stopped cooperating with my therapists. I would *never* do my exercises, so they figured, you know, what's the point?

My brother was born when I was seven. I was jealous. I was always very jealous. He was fine, and he could do a lot of things. I was eighteen before I could even cross a big highway by myself.

I went away to college—at Cazenovia, in upstate New York. It was hard at first. It was lonely. But I got really involved with people in my dorm and my classes; building relationships. Eventually, I took whatever art courses I could figure out. I stayed away from the fine arts; I took some independent courses in collage-making. Then later, I took a course in weaving. It always seemed like such a romantic art! So I learned it there, and I've kept it up for a long time. It just feels like something that belongs to me, that I can do whatever I want with. Although weaving can be very traditional and have very rigid rules, there's also a very fluid kind of structure. I learned to use big yarn and very textured material. There were no rules that I had to go by. There's a lot of room to explore and figure things out, and I wasn't finding that in other areas of my life. The art world seemed very endless and very open. I was very jealous when women would go off on dates and stuff. I wasn't shy, but it was the fact of being disabled. It's hard for young men to deal with that. The greatest problem is the attitude. People don't get enough information, and they make assumptions. People often think I'm mentally retarded because of my speech. Sometimes when I would try to explain, people would nod and go "uh-huh, uh-huh." I'd ask *them* a question, and they'd go "uh-huh, uh-huh." That frustrated me very much. People aren't real honest about disability. And that scared me. I would have to guess what a person was thinking, and try to respond. I went through a period of asking people, "Well, how do you feel about my disability?" They'd get kind of embarrassed— "Oh, you know . . ." So it was a struggle figuring out how to talk to people.

I met Earl in Washington, where I'd gone after the women's school in upstate New York. I lived on Dupont Circle and had a great roommate. I met Earl in a poetry group. He saw me trip and fall one day, and he was impressed that I picked myself up. We started spending time together, and he was a very free spirit. He did not want a commitment at all. But somehow we stuck together. It hasn't always been easy, but somehow we decided to work through that.

Earl Shoop:

I was really impressed when she tripped and got up. I think everybody's psychic to some degree, and I had this feeling that this person was going to play a big role in my life when I first saw her. So it wasn't surprising later on, when I saw her in the poetry group. We started, after the group, to go to her apartment to read some more poems. There was a certain amount of decorum that had to be followed—or protocol, whatever the word is.

I don't recall it being like a protective thing. I guess I think that if I had fallen down on the sidewalk, I would have felt embarrassed. It didn't seem to me that she exhibited signs of embarrassment about it . . . just a part of life, and keep on going.

About two months after we started seeing each other, there was a fire in my house—on St. Valentine's Day. My room got burned out. So she offered me space in her apartment until I could get myself together to find another place. It was sort of like the spider and the fly! She counted on my being lazy, and she was right.

Laureen Summers:

Then three years later we decided to get married. We had a really nice wedding in the country on a hill, up on a naked hilltop. We waited a long time before we decided to have a child. Mostly I didn't feel ready. I think—this is awful to say—but I just didn't have the skill. I thought I would abuse a child. I didn't want to take that chance. Then we both got involved in something called "reevaluation counseling"—a process of cocounseling—the basic theory being you've got to get your feelings cleared away so you can think better and proceed to act. I was asked to look at all my fears.

I remember the biggest negative reaction to my pregnancy coming from a woman priest whom I met at a party. "You don't want to do that!" Later I found out my relatives had said a couple of things. The people who best supported me, besides Earl, were the people at work.

It was interesting. I used to tell "dead baby" jokes, you know, and just talk about what I was scared of. When I was pregnant, the more the pregnancy advanced, the more relaxed I got. I thought I'd be in a wheelchair. I was very excited. I was really ready to have a child and go through pregnancy. It does make you believe in the state of mind affecting the body. When I feel bad about myself, the symptoms progress. When I'm confident, it shows. So it's interesting because there's been some talk about what part of any disability is emotional—and how much does that create a progressive disability.

By the time Melanie was born, I felt in great shape. I had an epidural, but I pushed her out and we got to hold her right away. It was great. I nursed her for ten months. I told her about my being disabled when she was a week old! She handles it well. She'll say, "Oh, Mommy, you can't do that—you shake too much." Things like that. But we've had some nice talks about how we both wished I didn't shake.

When you see people trying really hard to do the right thing, say the right thing, be the right thing—sometimes that makes it a little harder. We want so much to impress each other. We want each other's approval. So how could you judge someone who's really scared to talk about feeling embarrassed when with a mentally retarded child. "I don't want them touching me, I don't want to see them slobbering." My daughter is going through a lot of embarrassment right now. It's very hard. She's six and a half. We're very close, so it's confusing. We'll cuddle in the morning and all that, but then it's "Don't go into school with me. I can go alone. . . . Don't push the cart in the grocery store because you make it shake." So we're trying to find a way to deal with it. It's hard for her. We were talking about it last night, and how she doesn't like my shaking. She uses the words, "I feel embarrassed when people see you shake." So we just keep talking about it.

She's not embarrassed to have friends home. That's the confusing part. All the kids in the neighborhood drop in at our house. They come over, and that's fine. I think it's more going into places where people don't know me. She doesn't want to talk about it to people. I've asked her, "Well, why don't you just tell people I have cerebral palsy." Sometimes she does, but often she just does not want to deal with it.

The best thing is to do it your way. Work situations have not been great in that way. I'm in the process of trying to find myself a good professional position where I don't get intimidated, where I feel like I can use what I know, and where I'm involved in decision- and policy-making.

I let go of my weaving when Melanie was born, but my studio is all set up for me to go back to it. That's really important. I get a little weirder when I'm away too long from weaving or writing. It kind of keeps me balanced. I've been very, very angry about being disabled. And it's come out inappropriately. Mostly on poor Earl. But being an artist has also brought reassurance to me. I remember that I *am* an artist, and I *am* creative, and I *can* change things, and I *can* get what I want. The possibilities are endless.

My latest interest is working with parents who are disabled and figuring how to support them. When people have a chance to find their creativity—what they love to do—things fall into place.

Earl Shoop:

At the time we started that, she had been at some kind of group-encounter thing where everybody just trashed her—a destructive kind of thing. When she started in co-counseling, it was much better. I could see within a couple of weeks that she was very different. I'd come home and she wasn't crying! She solidified some of the things she wanted to do, and knew that she could. She decided she wanted to ride a bicycle!

Well, knowing for myself what was involved in learning to ride a bicycle, I thought it would be appropriate for her to learn a little bit more about balancing. So I got a beam for her, to put on the floor of the apartment, and she'd walk on it.

Then a friend, who was also involved in co-counseling, had a bicycle. We found a short, one-block, one-way street that didn't have a lot of traffic on it. My wife would get on the bicycle and just stand there straddling it, shaking, getting her nervousness out, then trying for a little while, then going into deep depression, getting back up on it again. After a while she got so good that we got her a bicycle. It was a small one, so she wouldn't have far to fall! I used that bicycle sometimes myself, until it got stolen. But she learned how to ride it well enough that it certainly gave her a lot more confidence in her ability to do things. It was a goal she set up and then accomplished. Later on, out in the country, visiting friends, she suddenly said, "I think I could drive." So I'd let her drive—driving into ditches, "I can't drive!", and so on, and so for a long time she didn't think about that anymore, until just this past year we decided she could do it. She scouted around and found a good driving instructor who taught physically disabled students.

Laureen Summers:

I got my driving license a month ago.

Earl Shoop:

She has a hard time not showing her emotions. When we visited her folks, we used to sit around playing penny-ante poker. When she had a good hand, everybody else would drop out right away, because they could see by the look on her face! "Oh, Laurie's got a full house or something!" So she hasn't quite developed a poker face or anything.

Laureen Summers:

Figure out what you know you want to do, and do it. Find a way to do it. You get in trouble when you try to please everyone but yourself. That doesn't mean at all that you don't respect people or listen to them, but while you're doing that, think of what you want, what's important to you, or is going to make *you* feel good. Then figure out what you need to do to get it done. As long as no one gets hurt, and you can figure out how to have good relationships so you get support for what you're doing, that is what makes people powerful. Building support, figuring out what you want, and going after it.

Somewhere in all of that, I got interested in Very Special Arts. I began to look at what was going on, and seeing that when children were allowed to participate in the kinds of arts programs that would let them explore and do what they wanted, they were being given an opportunity that wasn't available to them elsewhere.

I went there to work part time and did filing and copying. Then I graduated to being a special projects assistant. I got a chance to travel and see different programs, and I began to talk about the arts. It's funny. I'm still evolving. And it's nice.

When disabled people—people with disabilities, that's the

"correct" term, I guess—get involved with hands-on art, it's a very empowering experience. The arts afford us the opportunity to really express and create. What we dream about, what we think about. Plays are written from people's experience—from what people think about. Other people get to see them!—which must be a very powerful feeling. Pictures, weaving, dance, whatever—there is something in every form of art that comes out of people's dreams. For people like myself, it's very enriching to find a way to really get across to others what we think about or want. You can't do it if you give someone a coloring book and say, "Color the trees green and the sky blue." But if you give someone paper and paint and crayons and say, "Why don't you experiment and see what kind of design you can make, or lines you can draw?"—you're opening up a whole world for people. You're saying, "I want to know *you* through this art. I will be here to help you keep exploring." Because some people will need help. They will need you to show them colors, and they need to hold your hands. I'm thinking of severely disabled people, too. There's a way to get anyone to be creative, by virtue of the fact that all people dream; all people have thoughts, but they don't always find a safe way to communicate them.

We want people without disabilities to see the joy and the hope and the dreams that disabled people have, like anyone else, so that the disability is only a separate thing. It doesn't mean that someone's whole life is terrible, that someone has to be taken care of in every way. The arts give me hope: they warm and uplift me.

A lot of people with disabilities are very involved with getting things done—like passing the Americans with Disabilities Act. Until the bill was first introduced, with the exception of Senator Edward M. Kennedy, Senator Tom Harkin, Mr. Tony Coelho, managing director, Werthein, Schroder & Co. (former New York congressman), and a small group of other people, I think there was little awareness of how crucial the issue was for disabled people. Now you see disabled people in many more areas of life than you used to. And some can be very talented. True, there are stories almost every day of social workers and guidance counselors telling people they can't do very much, but that is starting to be challenged. In the last ten years disabled people have really begun to recognize that they have rights, can make their dreams come true, can have a say in what's being planned for them.

■

MARY VERDI-FLETCHER

Mary conducts a dance workshop for young children once a week at a studio in Cleveland. I watched with Bob, her husband of eleven years, while Mary led the children through their paces with quiet understanding, patience, and an infectious laugh. She regards her wheelchair as a "vehicle of freedom rather than confinement," and enjoys what she calls the "fluidity" of it. She is very satisfied with her life, because she is doing something that makes a difference to people—especially children. Mary feels there is much to be learned through the arts—freedom of expression, development of self-esteem, and the enhancement of creativity. "My great satisfaction in life is the knowledge that my love for music and dance is being handed down to others."

I was born with a disability called spina bifida. A disability from birth, it's a weakness of the spinal column. When I was growing up, I was able to walk with braces and crutches, but as I grew older I began to have serious problems. Although I have always had tremendous upper-body strength, I had no balance to speak of. I broke a leg a few times because I was so active. I've been in a wheelchair from the time I was twelve.

My parents were very supportive. I come from a very close Italian family, so I grew up among my cousins, a couple of us living together in one household. My mother was so concerned about my education that for eight years she really sacrificed by taking me to a parochial school for all able-bodied children; it was not integrated at that time. Every day, she had to carry me up flights of stairs so I could be there with children.

My father is more quiet; he's very protective. Once I graduated from school, both my parents became very protective, very much afraid of letting me pursue my own personal goals. They were afraid of the outcome once I was away from their protection, that since "This is a hard, cruel world" I might get hurt in the process. I've always said that I have three strikes against me: I was born female, disabled, and Italian. It was a very hard struggle to become truly independent because of my family situation—yet their caring was out of love, not out of any kind of possessiveness.

Fortunately for me, both my parents were involved in the arts—my mother had been a professional dancer, and my father a musician—so my interest in the arts really grew out of their stories, the pictures, and the newspaper articles they had saved over the years. They had actually met onstage. My mother was involved in a dance team with her sister (this was in the vaudeville days), and my father played for their performance one evening. They always say they met over the song "Stardust." My father had some heart problems, so he had to quit traveling a few years ago, and my mother quit dancing when she had children.

I had no difficulty associating with other children. But I did have episodes where I was hospitalized for extended periods of time. I've had ten major operations. Two of them were specifically on the spina bifida area. The first was when I was five weeks old. Another was related to the skeletal problem—I had a hip out of socket, and they operated to put it back in. I spent three months in a body cast as a result of that surgery—and it didn't work. I was seven years old.

Then I had problems with acute decubitus—bedsores. At one point, when I was twelve years old, I almost died from that. I was in hospital a month. I had eight boyfriends leave me at that time, and I nearly died from *that*!! But then, I think all of those episodes made me stronger. Having to experience such things as a child makes you mature a lot faster. You realize a lot of things. You see a lot of sickness, a lot of pain around you—not necessarily in yourself, but you see it in other people because you're in the hospital. I was around adults a lot more than other children. You gain a lot of understanding of people and of yourself when you're lying in bed and not able to move—you have a lot of time to think. All those elements help you to become much more—not centered exactly, but to know yourself.

I grew up in a very religious household. My grandmother, to whom I attribute much of my success, recently passed away. She was a very strong woman, very religious, much stronger than my parents in her determination for me, praying when people thought that I was going to die. She was an example of strength for me. She accomplished a great deal in her life. She came over from Europe and put her daughters in show business, watching over them and protecting them when they got into trouble along the way. She and her husband, even though we weren't wealthy, purchased a twenty-eight-room mansion in Cleveland to help bring her family together. Rather than leaving us money in her will, she took us all to Europe years ago, when we were about ten, so that we could track our own history. She thought that was more important, something we would always remember. I wasn't in a cast at that time. But I was very small—I only weigh sixty-five pounds now—so it was easy for my mother to carry me.

I'm a very directed person, very likely because of my grandmother. What I'm involved in now is what I have always pursued. I've always had a love of the arts, a desire to perform, and a great desire to bring joy and enthusiasm to others.

I started dancing ten years ago. I was in a wheelchair. My parents and I had moved from Cleveland into a suburban area—way out. I had met some people at the "dance fever" time—when John Travolta was in. *Everybody* was doing partner dancing. We would watch those shows on television. Some of my friends got together and my involvement really just came as a result of that. We decided I could do some of the very same moves in partnering as able-bodied people could. At that time we did it for fun. Then I moved back to Cleveland on my own and started working at the Independent Living Center. There I met a friend of mine with whom I had gone through high school. Her husband was an excellent dancer. He and I started doing some of the partnering. We would go out to the dance halls together and dance for fun. People began commenting on our partnership, how well we worked together; they were pretty astounded at what they were watching. In the greater Cleveland area, no one in a wheelchair had, at that time, gone out and danced. Just then, the national TV show *Dance Fever* competitions were traveling around from state to state, auditioning individuals to be on their show, and they came to Cleveland. People encouraged *us* to audition. They felt we'd make a good team. So we tried out. We were the first able-bodied/disabled dance team to compete. It really shook the producer. As I recall, we performed before a thousand people or so in this club. When I got onstage, there was a major hush. You could tell people were thinking, "What is a person in a *wheelchair* doing in a dance competition?" But once we had gotten into our dance piece (we incorporated some acrobatic stunts utilizing the wheelchair), we got a standing ovation when we finished. What had happened was that, after the first few seconds, the audience really forgot that I was in a wheelchair; it really saw that we were dancing together as partners. So they began looking at the costumes, at our interpretation, the choreography in terms of the music. And that was the start of Dancing Wheels. Because of that first performance, we got a lot of media attention throughout Cleveland. We began receiving requests to do performances for various groups, both disabled and nondisabled. We got a corporate sponsor interested in making us a special wheelchair. Originally the wheelchair was just an ordinary model. One was made for us that was weighted in the front; it was of stainless steel, and the chair would hold my partner, and when we did acrobatic stunts it wouldn't topple over. We've evolved so that now we can emphasize the art form, whereas, before, we were a novelty.

What I do is really difficult to describe. You have to see it. Our form of dance does not differ that much from able-bodied dancing, except that I'm doing my movement on wheels, instead of on legs. The choreography is the same that able-bodied partners use, so that we're really synchronized in our movements. We're even involved in ballet now, with the Cleveland Ballet. All this means that we've been contracted to provide outreach and education into the community to show the diversity of dance and the ability of people with physical challenges. We visit various groups. We're heavily involved in the schools. We're connected with Young Audiences of Greater Cleveland and Very Special Arts Ohio. We've been asked to be their touring artists this year.

We're also involved now in developing longer pieces of choreography for mainstay performances. We also provide classes for people with disabilities, specifically people in chairs who are interested in learning the Dancing Wheels method of dance, and later possibly to go on into advanced classes and become performance-ready.

We also present performances to large groups of able-bodied individuals, a lot of schools which are integrated, or exclusively able-bodied. It is important to bring the able-bodied community to the realization that people with disabilities can participate as artists and be recognized for their art forms. It is equally important for people with disabilities to be able to recognize that they too can participate in activities that in the past were thought to only be for the able-bodied community. Dance has always been something stereotypically people with disabilities thought was unapproachable to them. The Dancing Wheels motto has always been, "Whoever made up the rule that you can only dance on your two feet?" Dance is an expression, an emotion; it comes from within and can be demonstrated many different ways. We really hold true to that and I feel we're a prime example of it.

From the start I have felt a warmness and a welcoming from the arts community, a general acceptance because I'm involved in dance. I must say that when we approached the Ohio Arts Council last year for the first time as a nonprofit organization to pursue funding from the Dance Channel, it was amazing to sit through the process because it really opened our eyes. First of all, people have always welcomed a person with disabilities, but usually as a spectator. So they concentrate on the *front* of the theater, and their concern is that it's accessible to the disabled. Very often, no thought is given to the *back* of the theater, the stages, the dressing rooms, the entrance to the stage, and how they can be made accessible. That's because people with disabilities who are also performers haven't been recognized as actively as they should have been. I told the Dance Channel there was a controversy: Should this dance with wheelchairs be considered an art form? Does it have a real impact on the arts community? Or is it utilized only for recreation? They voted it in—a red-letter day!

Since then, the wheelchair manufacturer, Invacare, has become even more interested in supporting what we're doing—what we need to provide the opportunity for maximum movement and agility. We'll be receiving a chair shortly that will be dance-specific . . . with much smaller wheels and a combination of what's offered in other sports chairs. For people with disabilities, the manufacturers have really broken through with these sports chairs. They've designed a bowling chair which is really amazing! With my chair I'm able to go completely sideways. The chair backs are real low, so that one of the things my able-bodied dancers are working on is to lift me right out of the chair, to do the actual lifts that you would see in ballet. They always enjoy working with me because I'm very strong and lightweight. Those are the two things that make it easier. That is not to say that other aspects of dancing can't be done by other people. When you're choreographing, you need to keep the original type of movement, but accommodate it to fit different ability levels.

I think that dancing has helped my disability because there's constant movement; it has helped my strength and endurance. It helps me get around. I drive my car. I'm married—to an able-bodied person. I met him in a bar. It was when I was living in that small town outside of Cleveland. His friends owned the bar and they introduced us. They told me he was the smartest one of the whole group, so he and I should talk. He'd really had no experience with a person with a disability before. It didn't seem to affect him. We went together for three years, and we've been married now for six and a half years. We have not had children. I love children, and I'm surrounded by children all the time in the schools. I just feel that my life was very restrained for a long time when I lived at home, and that children would be an element that would restrain my activities again. I don't think that it would be fair to the child or myself to do that. I made that decision prior to getting married. My husband would probably like to have children a lot more than I would; but he understands where I'm coming from, and he's accepted that. It has never been an issue really. It wouldn't be fair to a child for me to continue this kind of work at the level I am. At this point in my life, it's more fast and furious, and it's stronger than it ever has been. I just feel that that's my direction in life.

A lot of people with disabilities—a lot of young adults—are very passive. I was very passive. I was always categorized as a very good child. I condone that, but I also think there is a point in time when you need to determine what you want out of life. Then you have to work very hard to reach those goals. Goals aren't easily attainable, and sometimes other people don't see them as being logical. Years ago if I would've said that I wanted to be a professional dancer and be paid for it, people would've sort of sneered, "Yeah, right." Of course, you need to know what *is* reasonable, but you also need to know that if you work very hard to attain those goals, you will one day achieve them. I am a very strong person, and I am very centered. I may have turned out that way disabled or not—although I think, as I said, that having been disabled from birth, being around adults, and around a lot of sorrow and pain and discomfort of others, taught me to live every moment to the max. I have no use for people who are lazy or don't use their talents. To me, they're the most disgusting people around. Or those who don't realize their own self-value and worth and are afraid of taking the chance. I don't have a lot of tolerance for people like that, which may be a fault of my own.

I was sitting back the other day—sometimes you can just get overwhelmed by the amount of work you have and the schedules to keep—and I wondered what it would be like for people who have no goals in life, who live their lives every day the same way, and wake up the next morning without something to do. I don't know if I could live my life like that. I have more of a fear that someday I won't have this. I don't even know how I would exist without being able to be a part of this.

APPENDICES

∎

Appendix 1

■

GLOSSARY

ACUPUNCTURE: A traditional Chinese therapeutic technique whereby the body is punctured with fine needles.

ACUTE ASTIGMATISM: Acute refractive defect of the lens that prevents the eye focusing sharply and distinctly.

AGORAPHOBIC: A person with an abnormal fear of open spaces.

ARTHRITIS: Acute inflammation of the joints, caused by infection, metabolic disorders, or constitutional weakness.

BIOFEEDBACK: A technique in which an attempt is made to consciously regulate a bodily function thought to be involuntary, such as blood pressure, by using an instrument to monitor the function and to signal changes in it.

BRACE: A device that steadies or supports a weight.

BRAILLE: A system of writing and printing for the blind in which raised dots represent letters and numerals (Louis Braille, 1809–52).

CEREBRAL PALSY: A condition caused by damage to the brain, usually occurring before, during, or shortly following birth. "Cerebral" refers to the brain and "palsy" to a disorder of movement or posture. It can range from mild to severe.

COMA: A deep, prolonged unconsciousness, usually the result of injury, disease, or poison.

COMPRESSION INJURY: A condition in which the brain is compressed by fractures, tumors, blood clots, abscesses, etc.

CONGENITAL: Existing at birth, but not hereditary.

DEAF: The inability to hear and understand conversational speech with or without a hearing aid.

DECUBITUS: Ulcerations of the skin caused by poor circulation brought on by immobility, often resulting in acute staph infections.

DISTAL JOINT: A joint at some distance from the point of attachment.

ELECTROMUSCULAR STIMULATION: The use of electricity to evoke a skeletal muscle response—used therapeutically to help those in whom the motor area of the brain does not originate movement on its own.

GENETIC: Relating to the origin or development of something affecting or affected by genes.

GLAUCOMA: A disease of the eye characterized by high intraocular pressure, hardening of the eyeball, and partial or complete loss of vision.

HYPNOSIS: An induced sleeplike condition in which an individual is extremely responsive to suggestions made by the hypnotist.

IRON LUNG: A chamber surrounding a patient's chest in which air pressure is regularly increased and decreased to induce artificial respiration.

JUVENILE RHEUMATOID ARTHRITIS: The most common rheumatic disease (a disease that causes joint pains and/or fever) to affect children. Children with this disease develop pain and swelling in one or more joints.

LAMINATE: Made up of thin layers of tissue.

LAMINECTOMY: Excision of the posterior arch of a vertebra.

MALIGNANT GROWTH: An abnormal growth that tends to spread.

METHADONE: A synthetic organic compound used as an analgesic and in treating heroin addiction.

MULTIPLE SCLEROSIS: A degenerative disease of the central nervous system in which a hardening of tissue occurs.

NYSTAGMUS: Continuous jerky, involuntary movements of the eye muscles. Dizziness and reduced vision are associated with this disorder.

OCCLUDED ARTERY: Obstruction to the flow of blood through an artery of the heart as the result of spasm of the vessel or the presence of a thrombus.

OPTICON: A reading device whereby a small camera is swept over words and vibrating pins simulate printed letters.

PARALYSIS: Loss or impairment of the ability to feel sensation in or to move a part of the body.

PARANOID SCHIZOPHRENIA: One catagory of a large group of severe disorders of unknown cause and usually of psychotic proportion, typically characterized by disturbances of language and communication; thought disturbances that may involve distortions of reality, misperceptions, and sometimes delusions of grandeur or persecution and hallucinations; mood changes and withdrawn, regressive, or bizarre behavior. These symptoms last longer than six months.

PARAPLEGIC: A person whose lower extremities and part of whose torso are paralyzed as a result of injury or disease of the spinal cord.

PARKINSON'S DISEASE: A progressive nervous disease of later life, characterized by muscular tremor, slowing movement, partial facial paralysis, and impaired muscular control.

PHENYLKETONURIA: PKU is an inherited disease characterized by the body's inability to properly metabolize phenylalanine. Chief symptoms of this enzyme disorder are mental retardation, seizures, and psychotic episodes.

POLIO: Poliomyelitis. A common acute viral disease characterized by fever, sore throat, headache, vomiting, often accompanied by stiffness of the neck and back. A major illness, characterized by involvement of the central nervous system, stiff neck, pleocytosis in the spinal fluid, and paralysis.

POLYARTICULAR: A form of juvenile rheumatoid arthritis defined as involving more than four joints. Arthritis predominates.

PSORIATIC ARTHRITIS: A distinct systemic disease in which psoriasis (skin disease characterized by whitish, scaly patches of varying size) is associated with inflammatory arthritis.

QUADRIPLEGIC: Also called a tetraplegic, a person paralyzed in the lower extremities, part of the torso as well as paralysis of the hands and partial paralysis of the arms.

RHEUMATOID ARTHRITIS: A constitutional disease of unknown cause and progressive course characterized by inflammation and swelling of joint structures.

SIGN LANGUAGE: A form of manual communication. American Sign Language is one form and has its own vocabulary, idioms, grammar, and syntax—different from English. The elements of this language consist of the hand shape, position, movement, and orientation of the hands to the body and each other. It also uses space, direction, and speed of movements, and facial expression to help convey meaning. Other methods of sign language include Signed English and Pidgin Sign Language.

SPINA BIFIDA: Cleft spine; an incomplete closure of the spinal column.

SPINAL CORD: A bundle of nerve fibers and cells that connect the brain with the muscles, skin, and internal organs.

STEROIDS: A combination of any numerous compounds, including the sterols and various hormones and glycosides.

SYSTEMIC: Of, relating to, or common to a system; affecting the body generally.

SYSTEMIC JUVENILE RHEUMATOID ARTHRITIS: Produces high fevers and rashes in addition to the joint involvement. It may affect the child's internal organs as well, including the heart and liver.

THALIDOMIDE: A drug formerly used as a tranquilizer; when taken during early pregnancy, it was discovered to be the cause of serious congenital anomalies in the fetus.

TUMOR: A confined mass of tissue that develops without inflammation from normal tissue, but has abnormal rate and growth and serves no function.

VERTEBRA: One of the bony or cartilaginous segments composing the spinal column.

VISUAL IMPAIRMENT: The consequence of a functional loss of vision. A person whose optimum visual acuity in the better eye is 20/200 is considered to have statutory or legal blindness. Visual impairments also include tunnel vision and color blindness.

ULTRASOUND: Vibrations of the same physical nature as sound, but with frequencies above the range of human hearing.

Appendix 11

■

DISABILITIES AWARENESS GUIDE

In the "Findings and Purposes" of the Americans with Disabilities Act (ADA) of 1990, Congress reported that approximately 43 million Americans have one or more physical or mental disabilities, and that this number is increasing as the population grows older. Congress referred to these people as a "discrete and insular minority who have been subjected to a history of purposeful, unequal treatment and relegated to an inferior status in our society." Congress further described the persistent discrimination experienced by people with disabilities in employment, housing, public accommodations, education, transportation, communication, recreation, institutionalization, health services, voting, and access to public services.

Congress reported that the severe disadvantages experienced by Americans with disabilities take many forms including:

- outright intentional exclusion;
- overprotective rules and policies;
- segregation or relegation to lesser services or programs;
- exclusionary standards; and
- architectural, transportation, and communication barriers.

The ADA was passed to address and eliminate the major forms of discrimination faced daily by people with disabilities.

The employment provisions of the ADA prohibit discrimination in all employment-related practices and activities. They are rooted in the legislative history of Sections 503 and 504 of the 1973 Rehabilitation Act, but are much more far-reaching. Additionally, there is much more awareness and involvement in the ADA by disability rights groups. The employment provisions became effective on July 26, 1992, and are expected to be rigorously enforced by the Equal Employment Opportunity Commission. Penalties for ADA employment discrimination, at a minimum, will include back pay, litigation expenses, and corrective action (e.g., hiring, reinstatement, promotion). In general, the public access provisions of the ADA became effective on January 26, 1992. They will be enforced by the Department of Justice, and civil penalties may reach $100,000 per violation.

The ADA, in conjunction with Section 504, is the most important civil rights legislation since the 1964 Civil Rights Act. It is leading to a major civil rights movement for Americans with disabilities, who have waited for decades to see their basic civil rights guaranteed by law.

Who are the 43 million Americans with disabilities? They are the largest and most diverse minority group in the U.S. Still, two thirds of their working-age members are unemployed even though 66 percent of these people say they want to work. According to the President's Committee on Employment of People with Disabilities, the cost to the American taxpayer is $300 billion annually. Worker compensation payments are over $25 billion per year, and one dollar of every hour of wages in America now goes for a disability-related expense. Disability is an equal opportunity phenomenon, affecting every racial and economic segment of our population.

To fall within the Americans with Disabilities Act's (ADA) definition of a person with a disability, a person:

- must have a physical and/or mental impairment that substantially limits one or more major life activities; or

- must have a record of such an impairment, or

- must be regarded as having such an impairment.

This definition is broad by design and is intended to address both medical and psychosocial impediments to the full integration of Americans with disabilities.

The ADA defines as disabled people who have completely recovered from a disabling condition, but who have a history or record of disability. People with a history of cancer, heart surgery, or mental illness are common examples. The ADA also defines as disabled people who once had been misclassified as disabled (e.g., a person with a medication allergy who may have been wrongly diagnosed as epileptic). People who may be regarded as having a disability include:

- a person with hypertension that is controlled by medication, but whose employer has decided he or she cannot do strenuous work;

- a person with facial disfigurement that is disabling only because of the attitudes and reactions of others;

- a person who is rumored to carry the AIDS virus, but who has no impairment and is disabled only by the perception of others.

These people receive the full protection of the ADA, guaranteeing basic civil rights.

Architectural and Communication Barriers

The ADA recognizes that one significant barrier is a person's physical access to and within the place where such services are provided. Inaccessibility primarily affects those with mobility and sensory impairments, but it is relevant to many other disabled and even nondisabled people (e.g., pregnant women and elderly people). Title III of the ADA specifies that discrimination includes a failure to remove architectural or communication barriers in existing facilities if such removal is readily achievable (i.e., accomplishable without much difficulty or expense). Examples would include modest adjustments such as adding grab bars in rest rooms, lowering public telephones, or adding Braille markings on elevator control buttons.

If the removal of a barrier is not readily achievable, then one must attempt to provide services or programs through alternate methods (e.g., providing assistance to retrieve items in an inaccessible location). The ADA mandates a much higher standard for "readily accessible to and usable by" regarding new construction and major alterations because it costs far less to design accessibility into a new construction project, typically adding 0.5 percent to 5 percent of the total budget.

Discrimination and Other Barriers

The lawmakers of the ADA were quick to recognize that the serious impediments to access for people with disabilities are not problems that can be solved solely by architects. They are problems of attitude. An attitudinal barrier is defined as a way of thinking or feeling that results in behavior which limits the potential of people with disabilities to function independently. Attitudes toward people with disabilities have been explored. Three important assumptions can be noted:

1. A small percentage of people have openly negative attitudes that are associated with prejudice, fear, ignorance, intolerance, insensitivity, discrimination, dislike, condescension, and the like. They subscribe to most of the myths surrounding disabilities, even in the face of documented evidence to the contrary.

2. The vast majority of the American public is neither positive nor negative toward people with disabilities. Their general reaction is one of massive and deliberate indifference. They just prefer not to think about disability at all.

3. This indifference is rooted in a perfectly natural psychological phenomenon in which, when we think about or encounter disability, we must think about and deal with the fragility of our

own health and ultimately our own mortality. To do so is unpleasant and uncomfortable for most people.

Avoiding this discomfort has been too expensive. Any indifference, unpleasantness, or discomfort felt, any attitudinal barriers that may have been erected around the issue of disability must be removed.

Suggestions to Improve Access and Positive Interactions

Offer assistance if you wish, but do not insist. Always ask before you act, but do not help without permission. If you are not sure what to do, ask the person to explain what would be helpful.

Focus on the abilities of the person, rather than on the disability. Be mindful that alternative ways of doing things are often equally effective. Encourage people with disabilities to be their own advocates.

Be aware of limitations specific to a disability, but do not be overprotective. Do not exclude the person from participating in an activity just because you assume their disability would be a problem. Let them make the decision; do not lower your expectations. There is dignity in being able to take risks. Allow a person with a disability to fail just as you would allow any other person. No one succeeds all the time.

Make sure that parking areas, rest rooms, and buildings in which you provide services or conduct meetings are architecturally and environmentally accessible to all people. This is crucial to the establishment of a comfortable and equitable relationship with people with a disability. Get expert advice before making expensive structural modifications.

Accessibility to the full range of services you provide is legally required. Review your programs and reading materials. Are they diverse enough to reach all levels of ability? Is the content accessible to people with hearing, visual, or learning disabilities (e.g., audiotapes, audiovisuals, large print)?

Conduct outreach efforts to publicize your programs to people

with disabilities. Allow time for them to become fully aware of your services and develop trust in your efforts.

Ask a person with a disability to facilitate disability awareness training sessions with staff to promote positive attitudes. Locate material and have it available for learning more about disability-related issues.

Involve people with disabilities on advisory boards, planning committees, in positions of authority, and in the planning and presentation of all sponsored programs. Actively seek qualified persons with disabilities when hiring for staff positions.

Assume responsibility for understanding the issues that affect people with disabilities. Learn more. Send for information from consumer and disability-related organizations, ask for their support, and invite their representatives to speak at meetings.

The Power of Language

It is important to monitor your use of written and spoken language regarding people with disabilities. Words are powerful tools, indicating the perceptions and attitudes of the person using them. The following general guidelines will be helpful:

1. Focus on issues and not on a disability. Above all, do not sensationalize a disability by using terms such as "afflicted with," "suffers from," "victim of," "shut-in," "infirmed," "crippled with," or "unfortunate." These expressions are very offensive, even defamatory, to people with disabilities.
2. Emphasize people, not generic labels. Say "people with mental retardation," not "the retarded." Put people first, not their disability.
3. Emphasize abilities, not limitations. Say "uses a wheelchair," not "confined to a wheelchair" or "wheelchair bound."
4. Avoid condescending euphemisms like "handicapped, mentally different, physically inconvenienced, physically challenged." These tend to trivialize disabilities and suggest that they cannot be dealt with in an upfront manner.
5. Avoid disease connotations such as "patients" or "cases."

MYTHS/FACTS

Myth: People with disabilities prefer to work with people who are disabled.

Fact: People with disabilities seek services from professionals who are the most qualified in their areas in terms of training, experience, knowledge of resources, and willingness to work with disability issues.

Myth: People with disabilities have interests, needs, desires, abilities, and lifestyles which are profoundly different from other people.

Fact: People with disabilities are more like than unlike people without disabilities in all respects. As with all of us, it is their unique individuality that makes each person different.

Myth: Disability is a constantly frustrating tragedy.

Fact: People with disabilities do not sit around and ponder their disability all the time. They simply carry out their lives as normally as they can.

Myth: People with disabilities prefer separate programs and services.

Fact: Most people with disabilities do not want or need separate programs which often limit opportunities and perpetuate segregation and the myth of "different-ness." Besides, the ADA expressly prohibits the provision of separate services "unless such action is necessary to provide a service that is as effective as that provided to others."

A LOOK AT ATTENTION DEFICIT DISORDER

Attention Deficit Disorder (ADD) is marked by developmentally inappropriate degrees of inattention, impulsiveness, and hyperactivity. ADD generally has an onset prior to the age of four. However, it is typical that ADD is not diagnosed until the child begins school. An estimated 3 to 5 percent of all schoolchildren experience ADD, and it occurs approximately six times more frequently in males than in females.

A common fallacy is that ADD is a learning disability. ADD is behavioral in nature and is characterized by impulsivity and an inability to remain focused on one topic. ADD frequently is accompanied by hyperactivity. In contrast, a learning disability is associated with how a person learns. School difficulties are common to both disabilities.

It is believed that ADD has a biological basis. This disability occurs more frequently in children from families with a history of developmental disorders, conduct disorders, and alcohol and other drug abuse.

Suggestions to Improve Access and Positive Interactions

Be patient when communicating with someone with ADD. Ask clarifying questions throughout the conversation to ensure that the person is grasping the information provided. Repetition will be necessary.

When communicating with a person with ADD, use innovative and unusual examples to catch the person's attention. Those with ADD tend to stay more focused when the information and modalities are presented in diverse ways.

Take frequent breaks. When the person seems to be drifting away from the lesson, take a break before refocusing on the topic at hand. People with ADD have the most difficulty in situations which require prolonged periods of attention.

People with ADD seem to stay focused better when in a structured setting, receiving frequent reinforcements. Important information may best be given in one-to-one situations.

MYTHS/FACTS

Myth: Attention Deficit Disorder is the same as learning disability.

Fact: These two disabilities can co-exist but each addresses distinctly different symptoms. ADD considers a person's inability to focus attention or control aspects of behavior. It frequently is accompanied by hyperactivity. Learning disability relates to specific developmental disorders associated with learning and learning modalities.

Myth: All people with ADD have brain damage.

Fact: Although some people with ADD do have signs of brain damage, the majority do not have measurable differences in brain function.

Myth: People outgrow ADD by the time they reach adulthood.

Fact: Approximately one third of the people with ADD experience continuing problems into adulthood, sometimes including conditions that adversely affect conduct.

A LOOK AT BLINDNESS AND VISUAL IMPAIRMENTS

A person whose optimum visual acuity in the better eye is 20/200 is considered to have statutory or legal blindness. It is estimated that 11.4 million Americans have some visual impairment, even with glasses. Of this number:

- 120,000 are totally blind;

- 600,000 are legally blind with some usable vision;

- 1,400,000 are severely visually impaired (cannot read newsprint with glasses).

Visual impairments also include tunnel vision and color blindness. Two thirds of blindness is caused by cataracts, glaucoma, diabetes, vascular disease, trauma, and heredity. One third is "cause unknown."

Suggestions to Improve Positive Interactions

To guide a person who is blind, let him or her take your arm. If you encounter steps, curbs, or other obstacles, identify them.

When sitting down, guide the person's hand to the back of the chair and tell him or her whether the chair has arms.

When giving directions, be as clear and specific as possible. Estimate the distance in steps, and point out obvious obstacles in the direct path of travel.

Speak directly to the person in a normal tone and speed. Do not shout or speak in a loud voice.

Resist the temptation to pet or play with a working guide dog. The dog is working and should not be distracted.

When leaving a room, say so. Anyone would feel foolish talking into thin air.

When the person who has a visual impairment must meet many people, introduce them individually. This helps the person to better associate names and voices for subsequent encounters.

Possible Solutions to Access Problems

- To facilitate mobility on a path of travel, remove displays or other objects; avoid clutter; use large-letter signs; raise low-hanging signs or lights.

- Written information is a problem. Try using talking calculators or computers. Increase the frequency of oral announcements; provide audiotapes or Braille transcripts of frequently requested information; have staff read aloud brochures or important information.

- Add raised or Braille lettering to elevator control buttons.

- Install entrance indicators such as strips of textured material near doorways, elevators, etc.

- Use radio for announcements and advertising.

- Have optical magnifiers and other optical aids available for the person with a visual impairment to use.

MYTHS/FACTS

Myth: Blindness means living in a world of darkness.

Fact: What a person is able to see depends upon the age of onset, degree of visual memory, and degree of usable vision regarding light, shape, etc.

Myth: All people who are blind read Braille.

Fact: Only about 10 percent read Braille, but there are many other assistive devices that promote independence. These include reading aids, listening aids, and readers.

Myth: People who are blind can hear and feel things no one else can; they have a "sixth sense."

Fact: Certain senses become more highly developed because people who are blind rely upon them more. There is nothing mystical about this phenomenon.

A LOOK AT DEAF/BLINDNESS

Deaf/blindness is considered one of the most debilitating forms of disability. The rubella epidemic of the 1960s resulted in a dramatic increase in the number of individuals experiencing deaf/blindness. Though that epidemic has long since passed, the need for services remains. Congress provides $15 million annually to the Helen Keller Center for Deaf-Blind Youths and Adults, a national resource to meet the direct service, training, and technological needs this population presents.

The federal government provides grants each year to state education agencies to assist in the cost of educating students with disabilities. Beyond this basic assistance (approximately $350 per eligible student) offered by the Individuals with Disabilities Education Act, PL 94-142, the government provides approximately $15 million in special purpose funds to support Deaf/Blind Projects. Deaf/blindness affects a very small percentage of the population who often require more intensive, more costly interventions. Regionally located Deaf/Blind Centers were believed to be a more economical, efficient service delivery model because of these low-incidence levels. As the field of disability has moved toward the integration of all students into the mainstream, the Deaf/Blind Centers have moved toward providing short-term direct service interventions; technical assistance; consultant services; and teacher training programs.

During the 1989–90 school year, 23,000 students between the ages of 6–21 were identified as eligible to receive services under PL 94-142 because of a visual impairment. An additional 1,600 students were identified in the category of deaf/blindness. Two thirds of the students with visual impairments received special education services either in a regular classroom or through a resource room program. The remaining one third were served in separate programs within the regular school or in a separate public or privately funded facility. The reverse was true for students with deaf/blindness, the majority of whom participate in programs offered in separate classrooms or facilities.

A LOOK AT DEAFNESS AND HEARING LOSS

Deafness is the inability to hear and understand conversational speech with or without a hearing aid. Hearing loss is a condition in which the sense of hearing is defective but functional for ordinary life purposes (usually with the help of a hearing aid). There are approximately 2 million persons in the United States who are deaf. Another 20 million Americans have some degree of hearing loss. These numbers are increasing due to the aging of the population and the exposure of young people to damaging noise levels, especially from music.

It is important to understand that the major handicap is not the inability to hear, but the difficulty in communication. The way in which the person with a hearing loss will communicate depends on these factors:

- degree of hearing loss;
- age at which the hearing loss developed;
- residual hearing;
- language skills;
- speech abilities;
- family environment;
- educational background.

The communication problems are more complicated for the person who never heard speech than for those whose hearing loss developed at a later age. Speech develops as we imitate others and listen to the sounds we make. To improve communication, a person with a hearing loss may rely upon lipreading, manual communication, teletypewriters, or pads and pens. All methods are acceptable, if communication is achieved.

More About Deafness

Society has enforced a communication barrier for people who are deaf. The communication problems were either ignored or the person with deafness was sent to special schools or institutions. As a result of this separatism, people with deafness began to form a culture among themselves. They employed their own means of communication and sought each other's company. Even today 80 percent of people who are deaf marry within their own culture.

It is important to learn at what type of school a person who is deaf learned communication skills. The different types include oral only schools and those using a total communication approach.

Oral-Only School: This type of school was developed by authorities to solve the problem of isolation of people with deafness. A strictly oral mode of speech training is enforced. Speech reading and vocal training are taught and sign language is forbidden.

Total Communication School: This approach was developed from the philosophy that the all-important goal was that a person who is deaf be able to communicate with anyone. Many leading teachers, including Thomas Gallaudet (for whom Gallaudet University was named), promoted this form of education. Sign-language skills were strongly advocated, along with whatever means aided communication, including speech reading, vocal training, and gesturing.

Sign language itself varies. American Sign Language (ASL) is growing in use. ASL is a subtle combination of hand, face, and body movements to comprise vocabulary and grammar that are distinct from English. It should be noted that very few hearing people learn to sign, further increasing the barriers around communication. Other methods of manual communication include Manually Coded English and Pidgin Sign English.

It is also important to note that, for the person who is deaf, English is a second language. The person may have difficulty understanding written or spoken English.

More About Hearing Loss

A person who has developed a hearing loss later in life may continue to use speech to communicate and may not use sign language. This person also may not associate with the deaf community or be involved in related activities.

The person with a hearing loss often relies on assistive listening devices, such as hearing aids, amplifiers, induction loops, etc. A hearing aid amplifies sound and can be beneficial for many, as long as some hearing remains. The aids help with volume but not necessarily with distinguishing sounds. Hearing aids require a period of learning and adapting and some people become sensitive to the amplified sound.

Suggestions to Improve Positive Interactions

Speak clearly and distinctly, but do not exaggerate or slow down unless asked.

Use a normal voice tone and provide a clear view of your mouth.

If an interpreter is involved, speak directly to the person with deafness—not the interpreter. Learn more about the role and proper use of a sign-language interpreter.

Ask the person to repeat if you do not understand. If that does not work, use a pad and pen. Achieving communication is more important than the method.

Avoid standing in front of a light source (e.g., window) which might silhouette your face, making it difficult to see.

Use facial expressions, body language, and pantomime.

Explain any interruption (phone rings, knock at door) before attending to it.

Learn how to find an interpreter on short notice.

Install a Telecommunication Device for the Deaf (TDD) in your reception area. Advertise its availability and learn how to operate it properly.

Encourage and support sign-language instruction for all interested employees.

Avoid such offensive terms as deaf and dumb, deaf-mute, or the deaf. Use persons with deafness or persons with a hearing loss.

Additional Suggestions for Group Meetings or Training Sessions

Assign someone to take notes, if an interpreter is not available.

Use a round or oval table to allow for a good line of sight to all participants.

Arrange for the person with a hearing loss to sit near the speaker in lecture situations.

Remind the lecturers to avoid pacing or talking with his or her back to the audience.

Maximize the use of visual aids, such as flip charts.

For a larger meeting, an induction loop could be used. This loop is a length of wire that is placed around the selected area (where people who have a hearing loss will be seated). The wire is connected to an amplifier and to the speaker's microphone. The magnetic field within the loop of wire is picked up by the telephone-switch setting on a hearing aid and changed to sound. This system can be used only by people who are able to use a hearing aid and have the telephone switch.

A new method of transcribing oral communication is Real Time Captioning. A typist, using a computer and special equipment, enters the speech or presentation and the text is projected onto a movie screen for participants.

Possible Solutions to Other Access Problems

- For information commonly obtained through telephones, provide small sound amplification devices or install a TDD. Also learn how to utilize the dual-party relay service that is provided by the local telephone company. This service allows for unrestricted communication between any person with a TDD and any person without one, day or night.

- Publish written notices of events that once were announced only orally. Arrange to have messages that are delivered by a public address system relayed in writing.

- Provide paper and pencils at work stations involving public contact.

- Install visual warning lights for fire and burglar alarms and doorbells.

- Allow mail-in procedures to be used to request information or respond to inquiries.

- Use visual cues for signage.

MYTHS/FACTS

Myth: All people with a hearing loss lack the ability to speak.

Fact: People who have lost their hearing after the development of speech have little difficulty speaking. Many persons with "prelingual" deafness have learned to use their voices in speech classes. This may present some initial difficulty for the listener to understand.

Myth: All people with a hearing loss can read lips.

Fact: Many people with a hearing loss have had formal training in lipreading. Even hearing people rely heavily on lipreading, but it is an imperfect process (about 30 to 40 percent accurate). It is rarely used in isolation of other communication methods.

Myth: Hearing aids totally correct hearing loss.

Fact: Hearing aids may improve hearing for many people with a hearing loss, but they are not corrective devices. It usually lessens the severity of the hearing loss.

Myth: Many people who are deaf have not even learned to speak. People who are deaf cannot be very bright.

Fact: It is extremely difficult to learn to speak if a hearing loss occurs before speech develops. Many other persons with deafness who have some speech have not mastered the fine grammatical points of their second language—English. The problem is one of communication, not intellect.

A LOOK AT HIDDEN DISABILITIES

People with hidden disabilities appear to be physically nondisabled, healthy, and productive, leading normal lives. They have "hidden" conditions such as cancer, epilepsy, diabetes, lung disease, kidney failure, hemophilia, hypertension, early stages of AIDS, or heart disease. Therefore most people will expect them to be totally self-sufficient and competent. Yet within the disability community, they do not feel like they belong—not "disabled enough" to fit into a group of active, assertive people with disabilities. Their numbers are far greater than those of any one disability group, but they are often in a state of limbo about belonging—feeling without a place in anyone's world. People with hidden disabilities are caught between not being fully accepted as a nondisabled person, yet not being recognized as someone with a "real" disability either.

The lawmakers of the Americans with Disabilities Act of 1990 (ADA) continued in the tradition of Section 504 and included people with hidden disabilities. This is demonstrated by the broad definition of disability which included persons with a history of impairment and those who are perceived as having a disability.

This is further reinforced by ADA regulations which encourage people with hidden disabilities to disclose their impairments and seek the full protection of the new federal law.

Suggestions to Improve Access and Positive Interactions

If you think that someone has a hidden disability, ask questions that may be appropriate to the treatment process. For example, "Is there anything about you we have not discussed that might make it difficult to participate in this program? Meet the program requirements? Engage in these physical activities?"

The removal of barriers and provision of reasonable accommodation for people with hidden disabilities is highly individualized. Sometimes the evidence of your genuineness and openness to more obvious disabilities will make people with hidden disabilities more likely to discuss openly the accommodation they require.

Provide an environment conducive to self-disclosure. This includes hiring people with disabilities; establishing a reputation for confidentiality; formally inviting employees and clients to self-identify; and providing descriptive literature and speakers regarding your interest in serving people with disabilities.

Once a person is identified as having a disability, an open and honest discussion can follow regarding the need for and nature of accommodation required. For most hidden disabilities, the primary accommodation required will be acceptance by the staff and clients.

Hidden disabilities are not contagious. Under the ADA, the Secretary of Health and Human Services will publish a list of contagious diseases each year and the conditions under which diseases may be transmitted. There is no reason to avoid people with disabilities for fear you might catch something.

MYTHS/FACTS

Myth: All people with cancer are dying.

Fact: Cancer is a large group of diseases characterized by uncontrolled growth and spread of abnormal cells. More than one third of people with cancer today are completely cured, and the others are living with cancer, not dying of it. Many cancers can be cured if detected and treated promptly.

Myth: Hidden disabilities, such as emphysema or cystic fibrosis, are contagious.

Fact: Hidden disabilities are not contagious, including respiratory problems accompanied by coughing or wheezing. Segregation makes the person feel abnormal and increases fear and misunderstanding.

Myth: Insulin cures diabetes.

Fact: There is no cure for diabetes, but insulin combined with exercise and diet can result in productive and healthy living despite diabetes.

Myth: People with epilepsy are likely to have seizures at any time.

Fact: Over 2 million Americans have seizure disorders and the overwhelming majority are controlled by medication. Many seizure episodes are as mild as blinking or a brief lapse of attention.

A LOOK AT LEARNING DISABILITIES

Learning disabilities are disorders manifested by significant difficulties in listening, speaking, reading, writing, reasoning, and mathematical abilities. The primary problems do not involve collecting information (as in sensory disabilities) but in interpreting, translating, or recalling information collected. Learning disabilities are intrinsic to the person, presumed to be due to central nervous system dysfunction, and may occur across the life span.

Learning disabilities range from mild to very severe. They affect between 5 to 10 percent of the population. There are many types of learning disabilities. Some examples include:

- dyslexia: severe problems with reading;

- dysgraphia: severe problems with writing;

- dysphasia: severe problems with speaking;

- dyscalcula: severe problems doing math.

Suggestions to Improve Access and Positive Interactions

Processing difficulties often interfere with learning. Extra time may be required to learn a certain skill. Once learned, however, there is no relationship between a learning disability and performance of the task.

Occasional inattentiveness, distraction, or loss of eye contact by the person with a learning disability is not unusual. Do not be concerned or offended, it is unintentional.

Some information processing problems may affect social skills, such as an unconventional or complete lack of response. Do not confuse this with rudeness.

A person with a learning disability sometimes has difficulty interpreting social cues (e.g., facial expressions, voice tone, and gestures). Accordingly, he or she may respond in an inappropriate manner. Again, do not confuse this with rudeness.

If future contact with a person with a learning disability is warranted, discuss openly the preferred way to communicate. This may be in writing or by phone.

Have your educational and promotional materials reviewed to see that they are available in various sensory modes and accessible to people with communication problems.

MYTHS/FACTS

Myth: Learning disability is just another name for mental retardation.

Fact: Both conditions interfere with the ability to learn. Mental retardation, however, involves a generalized, lowered intelligence while learning disability is specific to only one form of information processing. Learning disabilities, however, may occur in combinations.

Myth: A learning disability affects only academic achievement and disappears as a child matures.

Fact: A learning disability affects many aspects of a person's life such as driving, team participation, and human relations. Although its impact can be lessened somewhat as a person develops and learns to compensate, learning disability is usually a lifelong issue.

Myth: It is impossible to be both physically disabled and learning disabled.

Fact: Physical disabilities and learning disabilities occur independently of one another. A person with a physical disability is as likely to have a learning disability as a nondisabled person.

Myth: Learning disabilities are the result of other handicapping conditions or social influences.

Fact: Although learning disabilities may occur at the same time as other handicapping conditions (e.g., sensory impairment, emotional disturbance) or external influences (e.g., cultural differences, poor instruction), they are not the result of those conditions or influences.

Myth: Problems in self-regulatory behaviors, social perception, and social interaction constitute a learning disability.

Fact: By themselves these do not constitute a learning disability, although they may exist with a learning disability.

A LOOK AT MENTAL ILLNESS

Mental illness is a commonly occurring disability in the United States. Perhaps one third of the population will experience a mental disorder at one time in their lives. It is very difficult to determine the number of people with mental illness due to the nature of definitions. Mental illness often is considered a separate category from other disabilities, and this also confuses estimates of prevalence.

Two of the most common conditions are anxiety disorders and depression. There are different types of anxiety disorders, including:

- generalized anxiety disorder;

- panic disorder;

- post-traumatic stress disorder;

- obsessive-compulsive disorder; and

- social and other phobias.

Approximately one American in twenty will suffer at least one major depressive disorder in his or her life. Depressive illnesses include:

- major depression;

- dysthymic disorder;

- atypical depression; and

- manic depression.

Among the more severe forms of mental illness is schizophrenia. It is estimated that one percent of the population is schizophrenic. Unfortunately, only one half of these people are treated for the condition. Although mental illness is not considered a physically restricting condition, it is ranked ninth out of 67 chronic health conditions for causing activity limitation. Mental illness is included in the definition of disability in Section 504 of the Rehabilitation Act of 1973 and the Americans with Disabilities Act of 1990 (ADA).

Suggestions to Enhance Positive Interactions

Learn more about the nature of the person's diagnosed mental illness. If the person is prescribed medication for his or her illness, locate information on the side effects and long-term health impact.

Remember that people with mental health problems generally do not have lower intelligence. Some people may have difficulties with attention span or discussion topics that produce anxiety, but other communication problems should be minimal.

Be aware that people with more severe mental illness have difficulty dealing with emotions or expressing them. A person may smile even when he or she is angry or afraid.

Some people with mental health problems tend to overreact to emotionally charged topics or conversations. When this occurs, it is more likely that miscommunications will result. Important information should be conveyed in an objective manner, unless you know how the person is likely to react.

MYTHS/FACTS

Myth: People with mental illness are mentally retarded.

Fact: Most people with mental illness are average or above average in intelligence. During adjustment periods to medications, a person may appear lethargic. The medications do not affect intelligence.

Myth: People with mental illness are violent and dangerous.

Fact: Although some mental health diagnoses include symptoms of aggressive behavior, people with mental illness are no more violent than the norm.

Myth: People with mental illness never get better.

Fact: Most people with mental illness show improvement over time in their diagnosed condition. Some conditions, such as schizophrenia, usually are permanent; however, self-help groups, medication, case management, and psychotherapy can improve a person's quality of life and functioning level.

Myth: People with mental illness bring it on themselves.

Fact: Numerous research studies have shown that mental illness consists of bio-psycho-social conditions that are created by multiple factors. Some mental illnesses tend to recur in the same family.

A LOOK AT MENTAL RETARDATION

Mental retardation affects approximately 1 to 2 percent of the population, involving slightly more males than females. It refers to substantial limitations in certain personal capabilities. It is manifested as significantly sub-average intellectual functioning, and exists concurrently with related disabilities in two or more of the following adaptive skill areas:

—communications   —self-care
—home living   —social skills
—community use   —self-direction
—health and safety   —functional academics
—work   —leisure

It has been estimated that there are over 200 causes for mental retardation ranging from genetic disorders to environmental pollution. There are four levels of mental retardation—mild, moderate, severe, and profound, with most diagnoses falling in the mild category. Typically, an I.Q. score of 70 or below is indicative of mental retardation.

Mental retardation is often referred to as a developmental disability. The federal definition of a developmental disability is a severe, chronic disability of a person which:

• is attributable to a mental or physical impairment or combination of physical and mental impairments;

• is manifested before the person attains age 22;

• is likely to continue indefinitely;

• results in substantial functional limitations in three or more of the following areas of major life activity: self-care, receptive and expressive language, learning, mobility, self-direction, capacity for independent living, and economic self-sufficiency; and

• reflects the person's need for a combination and sequence of special, interdisciplinary or generic care, treatment or other services which are of lifelong or extended duration and are individually planned and coordinated.

This definition is interpreted differently at the state level. Disabilities such as brain injury, autism, cerebral palsy, and other neurological impairments may be included.

The degree to which a person with mental retardation adapts into society depends a great deal on early identification, family support, and appropriate education. Most people with mental retardation can function in jobs and live independently if appropriate educational and support services are available.

Suggestions to Improve Positive Interactions

Break down concepts into small, easy-to-understand components. Use concrete terms and avoid abstract ideas. Do not be afraid to explain concepts in logical steps in sessions that may be separated by hours or days.

Because of its social desirability, it is possible for a person with mental retardation to insist that he or she understands a concept when this is not true. When discussing or teaching a point, be certain that the person understands the concepts involved.

Avoid the tendency to talk around or about a person with mental retardation when that person is present. Direct questions or comments to that person, and allow him or her to seek assistance in answering if necessary.

If the communication deficits are significant, it may be helpful to involve an advocate in conjunction with the person with mental retardation. The advocate, someone who is familiar with the lifestyle and communication patterns of this person, can be of assistance in facilitating conversation or planning for needed services.

How Can I Get Involved?

Volunteer Organizations:

American Association on Mental Retardation, 1719 Kalorama Road, N.W., Washington, DC 20009, (800) 424-3688.

Best Buddies of America, Inc., 1350 New York Avenue, N.W., Washington, DC 20007, (202) 347-7265.

National Association of Retarded Citizens of the U.S., P.O. Box 6109, Arlington, TX 76005, (800) 433-5255.

Special Olympics, Inc., 1350 New York Avenue, N.W., Washington, DC 20007, (202) 628-3630.

MYTHS/FACTS

Myth: People with mental retardation cannot live independently.

Fact: Many people with mental retardation can achieve independence in daily living. Supervised housing also empowers some people with mental retardation to achieve independence.

Myth: People with mental retardation prefer to spend time around other people with the same disability.

Fact: Although it is natural to enjoy activities with peers, people with mental retardation also require and seek contact with people with normal intellectual functioning. The emotional states experienced by a person with mental retardation are identical to those of everyone else. Since expressive language is most impaired, other people tend to underestimate the emotional and social potential of the person with mental retardation.

Myth: All adults with mental retardation are childlike.

Fact: A person's developmental abilities are influenced by many factors, including the relationship with family and friends, school and work environment and the opportunities provided for growth and social development.

Myth: People with mental retardation are mentally ill.

Fact: A person with limited cognitive abilities can have the same range of emotional expression and emotional health as anyone else. People with mental retardation are most likely to behave inappropriately when there has not been access to environments which are supportive and successful.

A LOOK AT MOBILITY LIMITATIONS

A broad range of disabilities have the effect of restricting independent movement or travel. Problems with mobility may result from spinal cord injury, arthritis, muscular dystrophy, cerebral palsy, amputation, polio, stroke, breathing or stamina limitations, or other conditions. Over an estimated 25 million people have mobility problems, which may take the form of paralysis, muscle weakness, nerve damage, stiffness of the joints, or lack of balance or coordination. One million of these people are wheelchair users. Orthopedic impairments and arthritis affect 9.2 million people and rank as the top causes of activity limitations.

The Issue of Access

In reviewing your facility, office, or program's accessibility for people with mobility limitations, ask some of the following questions:

- Are paths and walkways at least 36 inches wide?

- Is parking conveniently located to a main building entrance via an accessible route?

- Is the carpet pile on the floor ½ inch or less?

- Are all rugs and mats securely fastened?

- Are there a reasonable number of (at least one) accessible toilet rooms on an accessible route?

- Are call buttons in the elevators located 42 inches or less above the floor?

This checklist is a sample taken from *Making the Workplace Accessible: Guidelines, Costs and Resources,* a 1990 publication of Mainstream, Inc.

Suggestions to Improve Positive Interactions

If the person appears to have little grasping ability, do not be afraid to try to shake hands. This is a traditional part of business etiquette, and signals that you are giving equal consideration. It is important to allow the person with a disability to guide you. He or she will have developed ways to handle almost all common social situations.

Do not hold on to a person's wheelchair. It is part of the person's body space and is both inappropriate and dangerous.

Talk directly to the person using a wheelchair, not to an attendant or third party. The person is not helpless or unable to talk.

If conversation becomes protracted, consider sitting down in order to share eye level. This not only is more respectful, but it may be more comfortable for both parties.

Avoid the following disabling terms: cripple, confined to a wheelchair, wheelchair bound, deformed, cord, quad, para. Use terms such as: person with (spinal cord injury, etc.), walks with (crutches, braces, etc.), wheelchair user.

Resources

The Spinal Network: the Total Resource for the Wheelchair Community. This directory and other publications are available from the Spinal Network, P.O. Box 4126, Boulder, CO 80306. Phone: (800) 338-5412.

National Resource Directory, an Information Guide for Persons with Spinal Cord Injury and Other Physical Disabilities. This directory can be ordered from the National Spinal Cord Injury Association. Their address is 600 West Cummings Park, Suite 2000, Woburn, MA 01801. Phone: (617) 935-2722.

DIRECT LINK for the Disabled, Inc., is a public benefit organization that provides information and resources for any disability-related question. Information packages about technology for people with disabilities; financial assistance; and notebooks of resources on stroke, spinal cord injury, or neuromuscular diseases are available. Write DIRECT LINK for the Disabled, Inc., P.O. Box 1036, Solvang, CA 93464. Phone: (805) 688-1603.

Possible Solutions to Access Problems

Make the necessary structural changes to eliminate barriers. Some suggestions:

- Add a ramp to cover one or two steps;

- Widen doorways;

- Lower towel dispensers in rest rooms;

- Lower telephones and water fountains;

- Make curb cuts in sidewalks and entrances;

- Use floor coverings that allow easy mobility (e.g., nonskid surfaces or low carpet);

- Add a paper-cup dispenser at a water fountain;

- Raise desks with blocks or use simple crank-style drafting tables as alternatives to standard desks;

- Replace existing hardware and equipment to allow for grab bars, handrails, and other supports where needed;

- Monitor access to emergency controls and general hardware (e.g., level door handles, light fixtures, vending machines), use "lazy Susans," which allow people to rotate equipment without reaching;

- Lower tension on doors and water fountains;

- Buy automatic electric staplers for paperwork;

- Attach items or equipment with Velcro;

- Relocate a program or service to an accessible area.

MYTHS/FACTS

Myth: All wheelchair users are paralyzed and are "confined" to their wheelchairs.

Fact: Many wheelchair users can walk with other mobility aids, but their speed, range, and convenience of movement is enhanced by wheelchair use. Wheelchairs liberate those who need them and confine none.

Myth: People with paraplegia are paralyzed from the waist down, and people with quadriplegia from the neck down.

Fact: Both paraplegia and quadriplegia are conditions with varying degrees of paralysis. A person with a high cervical injury may have total paralysis from the neck down, requiring the assistance of a respirator for breathing. Someone with a low cervical injury may have movement and control of the upper extremities except for the absence of finger grasp.

Myth: Accommodations for people with mobility limitations mean the complete removal of all architectural barriers.

Fact: The term "accommodation" covers a multitude of possibilities. Making worksite modifications, adjusting schedules, and acquiring specialized equipment are examples of accommodation. It is a highly individualized matter.

Myth: Accommodating a person with mobility limitations is expensive.

Fact: The overwhelming majority of accommodations (over 80 percent) cost less than $500.

A LOOK AT TRAUMATIC BRAIN INJURY

Traumatic brain injury refers to damage to the brain caused by external mechanical forces applied to the head. The traumatic brain injury (TBI) is acquired suddenly in the course of normal development. It typically results in brain damage which is diffuse or widespread; it is not usually confined to one area of the brain. Thus, impairments are multiple and many aspects of life are changed.

Someone receives a traumatic brain injury every 15 seconds in the United States. Over 2 million injuries occur per year, with 500,000 severe enough to require hospital admission. Between 75,000 and 100,000 people die each year from a traumatic brain injury, which is also the leading killer and cause for disability in children and young adults. The economic costs alone approach $25 billion per year, and astronomical medical and legal bills often leave families in financial ruin.

Among those who survive, 90,000 people will be severely and permanently disabled. They will experience deficits in physical, psychosocial, intellectual, cognitive, vocational, educational, recreational, and independent living skills. These deficits will vary in intensity over time, and will interact in ways unpredictable and unique. These interactions require extremely complex management and rehabilitation methods.

Suggestions to Improve Positive Interactions

People with TBI may digress or change course during a conversation. Redirect them, using appropriate cues and reinforcers.

Teach prevention skills to the person with TBI in more than one setting to maximize generalization. Focus on a specific prevention goal.

Be redundant. Never assume understanding or memory from a previous session. Always repeat the purpose, duration, and guidelines for each meeting. Summarize previous progress and then restate where the previous meeting left off.

It must be understood that because the consequences of TBI are so psychologically overwhelming, most persons experience pervasive denial. This is perfectly normal. The timing and method of confrontation about deficits, including alcohol and other drug problems, should be carefully coordinated with the interdisciplinary TBI treatment team and case manager. Present educational points in the most effective cognitive and sensory mode. This information is best obtained from a TBI team member known as the Cognitive Specialist.

All interventions should be directive in nature, short term, goal directed, and behaviorally anchored.

Severe brain injuries are typically so devastating to the family system that many family members "leave the field" when they come to appreciate what has occurred. Social isolation is common for people with TBI. The family system must be assessed and reassessed as it will fluctuate markedly in the first four years following TBI.

Accentuate positive gains, using frequent social praise.

MYTHS/FACTS

Myth: Most people with a very severe TBI will likely die.

Fact: Because of advances over the last two decades in emergency room medicine, neurosurgical techniques, and pharmacological agents, the survival rate for people with severe TBI has quadrupled to nearly 60 percent. Most are young adult males who will live a full life span.

Myth: Brain damage is permanent and irreversible. Life after TBI is not worth living.

Fact: There is a period of spontaneous neurological recovery of about two years in which significant improvements occur. These can be sometimes augmented by extensive and expensive rehabilitation methods. Some people with severe TBI will eventually live independently and work competitively with supports, but rarely at the level of functioning they enjoyed prior to injury.

Myth: People with TBI are volatile, aggressive, and unpredictable.

Fact: Almost all people who have experienced severe TBI pass through a phase of agitation during their recovery. This is normal and must not be confused with a permanent psychiatric condition. Behavioral problems that do linger for a minority of persons with TBI will likely include confusion, disinhibition, and/or reservation as opposed to aggression.

Myth: People with TBI experience dramatic losses of intellectual functioning.

Fact: There is usually some loss of intellectual functioning, but this can be confused with more specific cognitive deficits such as problems in attention/concentration, short-term memory, or the speed of information processing. These are often the most significant impediments to long-term recovery.

Myth: Most TBIs occur among people who were drinking and driving.

Fact: About two thirds of TBIs involve motor vehicle accidents. Half of the accidents which resulted in TBI are alcohol-related. Even in these circumstances, the people incurring TBI were often passengers or not intoxicated themselves. Falls, work-related accidents, sports-related injuries, and firearms account for many head injuries.

Myth: The point of impact and force of a TBI tells us a great deal about its consequences.

Fact: Most brain injuries are diffuse (affecting the whole brain and brain stem) and are not localized. The combinations and permutations of damage to over 10 billion interdependent nerve fibers are almost infinite, as are the manifestations of TBI.

Appendix 111

■

DISABILITY ORGANIZATIONS

Adaptive Environments Center, 374 Congress Street, Suite 301, Boston, MA 02210. (617) 695-1225 Voice and TDD.

AIDS Information (Hotline) (800) 342-2437, (800) 243-7889 TDD.

Alexander Graham Bell Association for the Deaf, 3417 Volta Place, N.W., Washington, DC 20007. (202) 337-5220 Voice and TDD.

American Academy of Otolaryngology/Head and Neck Surgery, 1 Prince Street, Alexandria, VA 22314. (703) 836-4444.

American Amputee Foundation, P.O. Box 55218, Hillcrest Station, Little Rock, AR 72225. (501) 666-2523, (800) 553-4483.

American Association on Mental Retardation, 1719 Kalorama Road, N.W., Washington, DC 20009. (202) 387-1968, (800) 424-3688.

American Cancer Society, 1599 Clifton Road, N.E., Atlanta, GA 30329. (800) ACS-2345.

American Council of the Blind, 1155 15th Street, N.W., Suite 720, Washington, DC 20005. (800) 424-8666, (202) 467-5081.

American Diabetes Association, 1660 Duke Street, Alexandria, VA 22314. (800) 232-3472.

American Foundation for the Blind, 15 West 16th Street, New York, NY 10011. (212) 620-2000.

American Heart Association, 7320 Greenville Avenue, Dallas, TX 75231. (214) 373-6300.

American Lung Association, 1740 Broadway, 14th Floor, New York, NY 10019. (212) 315-8700.

American Parkinson's Disease Association, 60 Bay Street, Suite 401, Staten Island, NY 10301. (718) 981-8001, in California (800) 908-9951.

American Psychiatric Association, 1400 K Street, N.W., Washington, D.C. 20005. (202) 682-6000.

American Society for Deaf Children, 814 Thayer Avenue, Silver Spring, MD 20910. (301) 961-8805.

American Speech-Language-Hearing Association, 10801 Rockville Pike, Rockville, MD 20852 (301) 897-5700, Voice and TDD.

Arthritis Foundation, 1314 Spring Street, N.W., Atlanta, GA 30309. (800) 283-7800.

Association of Birth Defect Children, Orlando Executive Park, Suite 270, 5400 Diplomat Circle, Orlando, FL 32810. (407) 629-1466.

Association for Children and Adults with Learning Disabilities, 4156 Library Road, Pittsburgh, PA 15234. (412) 341-1515.

Association for Persons with Severe Handicaps, 7010 Roosevelt Way, N.E., Seattle, WA 98115. (206) 523-8446, (206) 524-6198 TDD.

Association for Retarded Citizens, P.O. Box 1047, Arlington, TX 76006. (817) 261-6003, (817) 277-0553 TDD.

Barrier Free Environments, Inc., P.O. Box 30634, U.S. Highway 70, West Water Garden, Raleigh, NC 27622. (919) 782-7823.

Better Hearing Institute, P.O. Box 1840, Washington, D.C. 20013, Hearing Helpline, (800) 327-9355 Voice and TDD.

The Candlelighters Foundation, 1312 18th Street, N.W., Suite 200, Washington, DC 20036. (202) 659-5136.

Center on Postsecondary Education for Students with Learning Disabilities, University of Connecticut, Box 464, 249 Glenbrook Road, Storrs, CT 06269. (203) 486-4036.

Children with Attention Deficit Disorder, 1859 North Pine Island Road, Suite 185, Plantation, FL 33322. (305) 587-3700.

Clearinghouse on the Handicapped, Office of Special Education and Rehabilitative Services, Room 3132, Switzer Building, Washington, DC 20202. (202) 732-1245.

Council for Exceptional Children, Information Services, 1920 Association Drive, Reston, VA 22091. (703) 620-3660.

Cystic Fibrosis Foundation, 6931 Arlington Road, Bethesda, MD 20814. (800) 344-4823.

Deafness Research Foundation, 9 East 38th Street, New York, NY 10016. (212) 684-6556, (212) 684-6555 TDD.

Down Syndrome Congress, Dempster Street, Park Rodge, IL 60068. (708) 823-7550, (800) 232-6372.

Epilepsy Foundation of America, 4351 Garden City Drive, Landover, MD 20785. (800) 332-1000, (301) 459-3700 Voice and TDD.

Human Growth Foundation, 7777 Leesburg Pike, Falls Church, VA 22043. (703) 925-5534, (800) 451-6434.

International Polio Network, 5100 Oakland Avenue, Suite 206, St. Louis, MO 63110. (314) 534-0475.

JMA Foundation, 1730 M Street, N.W., Suite 903, Washington, DC 20036. (800) 447-8445.

Juvenile Diabetes Foundation International, 432 Park Avenue South, New York, NY 10016. (212) 889-7575.

Learning Disability Association of America, 4156 Library Road, Pittsburgh, PA 15234. (412) 341-1515.

Little People of America, P.O. Box 9897, Washington, DC 20016. (301) 589-0730.

Muscular Dystrophy Association, 810 Seventh Avenue, New York, NY 10019. (212) 586-0808.

National AIDS Clearinghouse, P.O. Box 6003, Rockville, MD 20850. (800) 458-5231.

National Alliance for the Mentally Ill, 2101 Wilson Blvd., Suite 302, Arlington, VA 22201. (703) 524-7600.

National Association for the Visually Handicapped, 22 West 21st Street, New York, NY 10010. (212) 889-3141.

National Association of the Deaf, 814 Thayer Avenue, Silver Spring, MD 20910. (301) 587-1788, (301) 587-1789 TDD.

National Association of Developmental Disabilities Council, 1234 Massachusetts Avenue, Washington, DC 20005. (202) 347-1234.

National Captioning Institute, 5203 Leesburg Pike, Falls Church, VA 22041, (703) 998-2400 Voice and TDD.

National Center for Law and the Handicapped, 1235 North Eddy Street, South Bend, IN 46617. (219) 288-4751.

National Center for Learning Disabilities, 99 Park Avenue, New York, NY 10016. (212) 687-7211.

National Chronic Pain Outreach Association, 7979 Old Georgetown Road, Suite 100, Bethesda, MD 20814. (301) 652-4948.

National Council on Independent Living, Troy Atrium, 4th Street and Broadway, Troy, NY 12180. (518) 274-1979, (518) 274-0701 TDD.

National Diabetes Information Clearinghouse, Box NDIC, 9000 Rockville Pike, Bethesda, MD 20892. (301) 468-2162.

National Down Syndrome Society, 666 Broadway, New York, NY 10012. (212) 460-9330, (800) 221-4602.

National Easter Seal Society, Inc., 70 East Lake Street, Chicago, IL 60612. (800) 221-6827, (312) 726-4258 TDD.

National Federation of the Blind, 1800 Johnson Street, Baltimore, MD 21230. (301) 659-9314.

National Head Injury Foundation, 1140 Connecticut Avenue, N.W., Suite 812, Washington, DC 20036. (202) 296-6443, (800) 444-NHIF (Family Help Line).

National Information Center on Deafness, Gallaudet University, 800 Florida Avenue, N.E., Washington, DC 20002. (202) 651-5109 Voice and TDD.

National Kidney Foundation, 30 East 33rd Street, New York, NY 10016. (212) 889-2210.

National Kidney and Urologic Diseases Information Clearinghouse, Box NKUDIC, 9000 Rockville Pike, Bethesda, MD 20892. (301) 468-6345.

National Mental Health Association, 1021 Prince Street, Alexandria, VA 22314. (703) 684-7722.

National Multiple Sclerosis, 205 East 42nd Street, New York, NY 10017. (212) 986-3240.

National Network of Learning Disabled Adults, 800 North 82nd Street, Suite F2, Scottsdale, AZ 85257. (602) 941-5112.

National Organization on Disability, 910 16th Street, N.W., Washington, DC 20006. (800) 248-ABLE, (202) 293-5960, (202) 293-5968 TDD.

National Rehabilitation Information Center, 8455 Colesville Road, #935, Silver Spring, MD 22091. (800) 34-NARIC Voice and TDD.

National Spinal Cord Injury Association, 600 West Cummings Park, Suite 2000, Woodburn, MA 01801. (800) 962-9629.

National Stroke Association, 300 East Hampden Avenue, Suite 240, Englewood, CO 80110. (303) 762-9922.

National Technical Institute for the Deaf, Rochester Institute of Technology, 1 Lomb Memorial Drive, P.O. Box 9887, Rochester, NY 14623, (716) 475-6400, (716) 475-2181 TDD.

Orton Dyslexia Society, Chester Building, Suite 382, 8600 LaSalle Road, Baltimore, MD 21204. (301) 296-0232.

Paralyzed Veterans of America, 801 18th Street, N.W., Washington, DC 20006. (800) 424-8200.

People First, P.O. Box 12642, Tacoma, WA 98401. (206) 272-2811.

Rehabilitation International, The International Society for Rehabilitation of the Disabled, 25 East 21st Street, New York, NY 10010. (212) 420-1500.

Self-Help for Hard of Hearing People (SHHH), 7800 Wisconsin Avenue, Bethesda, MD 20814. (301) 657-2248, (301) 657-2249 TDD.

Spinal Network, P.O. Box 4126, Boulder, CO 80306. (303) 449-5412, (800) 338-5412.

United Cerebral Palsy Association, 1522 K Street, N.W., Suite 1112, Washington, DC 20005. (800) USA-5UCP, (202) 842-1266 Voice and TDD.

GOVERNMENT AGENCIES

Administration on Developmental Disabilities, 200 Independence Avenue, S.W., Room 336D, Washington, DC 20201. (202) 245-2890.

Alcohol, Drug Abuse, and Mental Health Administration, U.S. Department of Health and Human Services, Rockville, MD 20857. (301) 443-3783.

Architectural and Transportation Barriers Compliance Board, 111 18th Street, N.W., Suite 501, Washington, DC 20036. (202) 653-7834 Voice and TDD.

Division of the Blind and Visually Impaired, Rehabilitation Services Administration, U.S. Department of Education, 330 C Street, S.W., Washington, DC 20202. (202) 732-1309.

National Cancer Institute, Building 31, Room 10A16, 9000 Rockville Pike, Bethesda, MD 20892. (301) 496-6631.

National Council on Disability, 800 Independence Avenue, S.W., Suite 814, Washington, DC 20591. (202) 267-3235, (202) 267-3232 TDD.

National Heart, Lung and Blood Institute, Building 31, 9000 Rockville Pike, Bethesda, MD 20892. (301) 496-4236.

National Information Center for Children and Youth with Disabilities, P.O. Box 1492, Washington, DC 20013. (703) 893-6061, (800) 999-5599, (703) 893-8614 TDD.

The National Institute on Deafness and Other Communication Disorders, National Institute of Health, Building 31, Room 3C35, Bethesda, MD 20892. (301) 496-7243, (301) 402-0252 TDD.

National Institute of Diabetes and Digestive and Kidney Diseases, Building 31, 9000 Rockville Pike, Bethesda, MD 20892. (301) 496-3583.

National Institute on Disability and Rehabilitation Research, U.S. Department of Education, 400 Maryland Avenue, S.W., Washington, DC 20202. (202) 732-1134, (202) 732-5316 TDD.

National Institute of Mental Health, 5600 Fishers Lane, Rockville, MD 20857. (301) 443-3673.

National Institute of Neurological Disorders and Stroke, Building 31, Room 8A06, 9000 Rockville Pike, Bethesda, MD 20892. (301) 496-5924.

National Library Service for the Blind and Physically Handicapped, Library of Congress, Washington, DC 20542. (202) 707-5100.

Office of Special Education Programs, Room 3086, Switzer Building, 330 C Street, S.W., Washington, DC 20036. (202) 732-1007, (202) 732-1170 TDD.

President's Committee on Employment of People with Disabilities, 1331 F Street, N.W., Suite 300, Washington, DC 20004. (202) 376-6200, (202) 376-6205 TDD.

President's Committee on Mental Retardation, Room 5325, Cohen Building, 330 Independence Avenue, Washington, DC 20201. (202) 619-0634.

Rehabilitation Services Administration, U.S. Department of Education, 330 C Street, S.W., Washington, DC 20001. (202) 732-1282.

ARTS AND DISABILITY ORGANIZATIONS

American Association for Music Therapy, New York University School of Education, Room 775, Washington Square, New York, NY 10003. (212) 598-1212.

Association of Handicapped Artists, Inc., 503 Brisbane Building, Buffalo, NY 14203. (716) 683-4624.

Deaf Artists of America, P.O. Box 18190, Rochester, NY 14618. (716) 244-8697 Voice and TDD.

Disabled Artists' Network, P.O. Box 20781, New York, NY 10025.

Famous People Players, 301 Landsdowne Avenue, Toronto, Ontario M6K 2W5 Canada. (416) 532-1137.

Hope University, P.O. Box 4818, Anaheim, CA 92803. (714) 778-8877.

Hospital Audiences, Inc., 1540 Broadway, New York, NY 10036. (212) 575-7660.

Kids on the Block, 9385-C Gerwig Lane, Columbia, MD 21046. (800) 368-KIDS, (301) 290-9095 in Maryland.

National Association for Music Therapy, Inc., P.O. Box 610, Lawrence, KN 66041. (913) 842-1909.

The National Institute of Art and Disabilities, 233 South 41st Street, Richmond, CA 94804. (415) 620-0290/0299.

National Technical Institute for the Deaf, Rochester Institute of Technology, 1 Lomb Memorial Drive, Box 9887, Rochester, NY 14623. (716) 475-6400, (716) 475-2181 TDD.

The National Theatre for the Deaf, P.O. Box 659, Chester, CT 06412. (203) 526-4971, (203) 526-4974 TDD.

Appendix IV

■

VERY SPECIAL ARTS STATE ORGANIZATIONS

Very Special Arts

Very Special Arts, an educational affiliate of the John F. Kennedy Center for the Performing Arts, is an international organization dedicated to enriching the lives of children, youth, and adults with disabilities through programs in the arts. Very Special Arts provides opportunities in drama, dance, music, literature, and the visual arts for individuals with mental and physical disabilities. Programs and training sessions are conducted in all fifty states and in the District of Columbia through a statewide network of local organizations. Very Special Arts at present extends to more than fifty-five countries around the world.

For information on how you can become involved with Very Special Arts in your area, please contact 1-800-933-8721 or call your Very Special Arts state organization:

ALABAMA
3504 Altabrook Drive
Birmingham, AL 35243
205-967-5093

ALASKA
P.O. Box 773185
Eagle River, AK 99577
907-694-8722

ARIZONA
3321 N. Chapel
Tucson, AZ 85716
602-795-6502

ARKANSAS
100 S. Main Street
Suite 459
Little Rock, AR 72201
501-374-5221

CALIFORNIA
29050 S. Western Avenue
Suite 101
San Pedro, CA 90732
916-891-0689

COLORADO
938 Bannock Street, #110
Denver, CO 80203-4029
303-595-9207

CONNECTICUT
56 Arbor Street
Hartford, CT 06106
203-236-3812

DISTRICT OF COLUMBIA
Trinity College, c/o Special
    Ed. Program
125 Michigan Avenue, N.E.
Washington, DC 20017
202-939-5143
202-939-5008

DELAWARE
University of Delaware
#012 Willard Hall
    Education Building
Newark, DE 19716-2940
302-451-2084

FLORIDA
P.O. Box 10453
Tallahassee, FL 32302
904-222-7742

GEORGIA
1904 Monroe Drive #110
Atlanta, GA 30324
404-892-3645

HAWAII
P.O. Box 88277
Honolulu, HI 96830-8277
808-735-4325

IDAHO
301 East 3rd Street
Suite 1, Room B
Moscow, ID 83843
208-883-8419

ILLINOIS
Delphi Special Recreation
    Association
305 Spring Bay Road
East Peoria, IL 61611
309-699-9052

INDIANA
1605 East 86th Street
Indianapolis, IN 46240
317-253-5504

IOWA
Department of Education,
  Grimes State Office
Building/3EN
Des Moines, IA 50319
515-281-3179

KANSAS
321 North Iuka
Pratt, KS 67124
316-672-7630

KENTUCKY
c/o Kentucky Department of
  Education
Capital Plaza Tower; 8th
  Floor
Frankfort, KY 40601
502-564-4970

LOUISIANA
2758-C Brightside Drive
Baton Rouge, LA 70821
504-765-2600

MAINE
P.O. Box 8534
209 Congress Street
Portland, ME 04104
207-761-3861

MARYLAND
6802 McClean Boulevard
Baltimore, MD 21234
301-426-0022

MASSACHUSETTS
China Trade Center
2 Boylston Street
Second Floor
Boston, MA 02116
617-350-7713

MICHIGAN
P.O. Box 1999
Royal Oak, MI 48067
313-546-9298

MINNESOTA
528 Hennepin Avenue #201
Hennepin Center for the Arts
Minneapolis, MN 55403
612-332-3885

MISSISSIPPI
P.O. Box 5365
Mississippi State, MS
  39762-5365
601-325-2367

MISSOURI
Behavioral Studies
  Department
8001 Natural Bridge Road
St. Louis, MO 63121
314-553-5752

MONTANA
46 North Corbin Hall
University of Montana
Missoula, MT 59812
406-243-4847
406-243-5467

NEBRASKA
West Center
University of Nebraska at
   Kearney
Kearney, NE 68849
308-234-8315
308-234-8314

NEVADA
200 Flint Street
Reno, NV 89501
702-329-1401

NEW HAMPSHIRE
Box 2338
Concord, NH 03301
603-228-4330

NEW JERSEY
841 Georges Road
North Brunswick, NJ 08902
908-745-3885

NEW MEXICO
P.O. Box 7784
Albuquerque, NM 87194
505-768-5188

NEW YORK
Margaret Chapman School
5 Bradhurst Avenue
Hawthorne, NY 10532
914-592-8526

NEW YORK CITY
100 East 42nd Street, Suite
   1850
New York, NY 10017
212-983-2965

NORTH CAROLINA
Department of Public
   Instruction
Div. of Exceptional
   Children's Services
116 W. Edenton Street
Raleigh, NC 27603-1712
919-733-3921

NORTH DAKOTA
ND Department of Public
   Instruction
State Capitol
600 E. Boulevard
   Avenue—9th Floor
Bismark, ND 58505-0440
701-224-4525

OHIO
Baker Hostetler
65 East State Street
Suite #2100
Columbus, OH 43215
614-433-9954

OKLAHOMA
P.O. Box 54490
Oklahoma City, OK
   73154–1461
405-521-3034

OREGON
P.O. Box 304
Salem, OR 97308-0304
503-378-3598

PENNSYLVANIA
212 Arts Cottage
Pennsylvania State University
University Park, PA 16802
814-865-5601/6507

RHODE ISLAND
500 Prospect Street
Pawtucket, RI 02860
401-725-0247

SOUTH CAROLINA
P.O. Box 575
Ladson, SC 29456
803-821-5849

SOUTH DAKOTA
300 North Dakota Avenue
Suite #602
Sioux Falls, SD 57102
605-339-4393

TENNESSEE
916 Robertson Academy
   Road
Nashville, TN 37220
615-269-5943

TEXAS
c/o Texas School for the
   Deaf
1102 S. Congress
P.O. Box 3538
Austin, TX 78764
512-389-7209

UTAH
P.O. Box 526244
Salt Lake City, UT
   84152-6244
801-328-0703

VERMONT
P.O. Box 1510
100 State Street
Montpelier, VT 05602
802-229-1503

VIRGINIA
P.O. Box 29081
Richmond, VA 23229
804-225-2070
804-225-4052

WASHINGTON
158 Thomas Street
   Suite #15
Seattle, WA 98109
206-443-1843

WEST VIRGINIA
University of West Virginia
   College of Graduate
   Studies
P.O. Box 1003
Institute, WV 25112

WISCONSIN
4797 Hayes Road, Suite 202
Madison, WI 53704
608-241-2131

WYOMING
1603 Capitol Avenue
Suite 205
Cheyenne, WY 82009
307-634-8812

Appendix ℧

■

VERY SPECIAL ARTS
NATIONAL PROGRAMS

In keeping with its mission to provide individuals with disabilities opportunities for lifelong learning through the arts, Very Special Arts offers programs in the arts for persons of all ages with disabilities. These national programs, conducted throughout the United States in cooperation with Very Special Arts state organizations, are offered in schools, hospitals, art centers, and other community organizations.

The **Artists Unlimited Project** brings artwork created by Very Special Arts participants to hospitals and other health-care institutions. The goal of this project is to improve the quality of life for patients and residents, and to heighten the self-confidence of individuals with disabilities who see their artwork lift the spirits of others.

The **Arts for Hospitalized Children** Medical School Course, piloted at Georgetown University School of Medicine and adopted by other leading medical schools in the United States, teaches medical students the value of utilizing arts activities with pediatric patients through hands-on experiences.

The **Native American Project,** supported by the Bureau of Indian Affairs, provides ongoing opportunities for Native American children with special needs to participate in the arts and in an annual festival.

New Visions Dance Project, developed in cooperation with the Alvin Ailey American Dance Center, teaches dance and creative movement to visually impaired children and adults.

Start with the Arts fosters the development of social and learning skills in young children through developmentally appropriate activities in music, dance, visual arts, and creative dramatics.

The **VA/Very Special Arts Program** provides opportunities for veterans with disabilities to participate in arts experiences that open avenues for creative expression, personal development, and lifelong learning.

Very Special Arts Festivals are conducted annually in communities throughout the United States. These fully integrated celebrations are held annually in each state and vary in size from state to state. The festivals provide a noncompetitive forum in which artists with disabilities share their accomplishments through performances, exhibitions, workshops, and demonstrations. An **International Very Special Arts Festival** is held in Washington, D.C., every five years. This month-long celebration to which the public is invited brings together more than 1,000 people from all fifty states and more than fifty-five countries to celebrate their accomplishments in the arts.

Very Special Arts Gallery is one of the first fully mainstreamed galleries in the country, representing emerging and recognized artists with emphasis on work by professionals with disabilities. It features works by many world-renowned artists, including Hiro Yamagata, Robert Rauschenberg, and Frank Stella. Proceeds from art sales benefit the national and international programs of Very Special Arts.

The **Young Playwrights Program** promotes understanding of disability issues in contemporary society by introducing students to the art of writing for the stage. Each year a student's script is selected and presented at the John F. Kennedy Center for the Performing Arts in Washington, D.C.

The **Young Soloists Program** annually presents an outstanding young musician with a disability with the Itzhak Perlman Award.

About the Authors

JEAN KENNEDY SMITH is the founder of Very Special Arts, an international organization dedicated to enriching the lives of individuals with disabilities through participation in the arts. Established in 1974 as an educational affiliate of the John F. Kennedy Center for the Performing Arts, Very Special Arts provides opportunities in drama, dance, music, literature, and the visual arts for individuals with mental and physical disabilities. Mrs. Smith is also a trustee of the John F. Kennedy Center for the Performing Arts and is a trustee of the Joseph P. Kennedy, Jr., Foundation.

GEORGE PLIMPTON is the editor of *The Paris Review*. He is the author of a number of books, many with a sports background, *Out of My League, Paper Lion, Shadow Box, Open Net* among them, as well as a novel, *The Curious Case of Sidd Finch*, and three co-edited works: *Robert F. Kennedy: An American Journey, Edie*, and *D.V.* His most recent collections include *The Best of Plimpton* and the *Norton Book of Sports*.

About the Type

This book was set in Sabon, a typeface designed by the well-known German typographer, Jan Tschichold (1902–74). Sabon's design is based upon the original letter forms of Claude Garamond, and was created specifically to be used for three sources: foundry type for hand composition, Linotype, and Monotype. Tschichold named his typeface for the famous Frankfurt typefounder Jacques Sabon, who died in 1580.